Foul Deeds and Suspicious Deaths In Warwickshire

FOUL DEEDS AND SUSPICIOUS DEATHS Series

Wharncliffe's *Foul Deeds and Suspicious Deaths* series explores, in detail, crimes of passion, brutal murders and foul misdemeanours from early modern times to the present day. Victorian street crime, mysterious death and modern murders tell tales where passion, jealousy and social deprivation brought unexpected violence to those involved. From unexplained death and suicide to murder and manslaughter, the books provide a fascinating insight into the lives of both victims and perpetrators as well as society as a whole.

Other titles in the series include:

Foul Deeds and Suspicious Deaths in Birmingham, Nick Billingham
ISBN: 1-903425-96-4. £10.99

Foul Deeds and Suspicious Deaths in Bolton, Glynis Cooper
ISBN: 1-903425-63-8. £9.99

Foul Deeds and Suspicious Deaths in and Around Bristol, Veronica Smith
ISBN: 1-84563-013-0. £0.00

Foul Deeds and Suspicious Deaths in Colchester, Patrick Denney
ISBN: 1-903425-80-8. £10.99

Foul Deeds and Suspicious Deaths in Coventry, David McGrory
ISBN: 1-903425-57-3. £9.99

Foul Deeds and Suspicious Deaths Around Derby, Kevin Turton
ISBN: 1-903425-76-X. £9.99

Foul Deeds and Suspicious Deaths in and around Durham, Maureen Anderson
ISBN: 1-903425-46-8. £9.99

Foul Deeds and Suspicious Deaths in London's East End, Geoffrey Howse
ISBN: 1-903425-71-9. £10.99

Foul Deeds and Suspicious Deaths in Hampstead, Holborn & St Pancras,
Mark Aston
ISBN: 1-903425-94-8. £10.99

Foul Deeds and Suspicious Deaths in Hull, David Goodman
ISBN: 1-903425-43-3. £9.99

Foul Deeds and Suspicious Deaths Around Leicester, Kevin Turton
ISBN: 1-903425-75-1. £10.99

Foul Deeds and Suspicious Deaths in Manchester, Martin Baggoley
ISBN: 1-903425-65-4. £9.99

Foul Deeds and Suspicious Deaths in Newcastle, Maureen Anderson
ISBN: 1-903425-34-4. £9.99

Foul Deeds and Suspicious Deaths in Newport, Terry Underwood
ISBN: 1-903425-59-X. £9.99

Foul Deeds and Suspicious Deaths in and Around Scunthorpe, Stephen Wade
ISBN: 1-903425-88-3. £9.99

Foul Deeds and Suspicious Deaths in Stratford and South Warwickshire, Nick Billingham
ISBN: 1-903425-99-9. £10.99

Foul Deeds and Suspicious Deaths in York, Keith Henson
ISBN: 1-903425-33-6. £9.99

Please contact us via any of the methods below for more information or a catalogue.

WHARNCLIFFE BOOKS

47 Church Street – Barnsley – South Yorkshire – S70 2AS

Tel: 01226 734555 – 734222 Fax: 01226 734438

E-mail: enquiries@pen-and-sword.co.uk – Website: www.wharncliffebooks.co.uk

Foul Deeds & Suspicious Deaths In

WARWICKSHIRE

J P Lethbridge

Series Editor

Brian Elliott

Wharncliffe Books

First published in Great Britain in 2007 by
Wharncliffe Books
an imprint of
Pen & Sword Books Ltd
47 Church Street
Barnsley
South Yorkshire
S70 2AS

ISBN 978 1 84563 003 4

A CIP catalogue record for this book is available from the
British Library

Typeset in Plantin and Benguiat by
Phoenix Typesetting, Auldgirth, Dumfriesshire

Printed and bound in England by
Biddles Ltd, King's Lynn

Pen & Sword Books Ltd incorporates the Imprints of Pen
& Sword Aviation, Pen & Sword Maritime,
Pen & Sword Military, Wharncliffe Local History, Pen
and Sword Select, Pen and Sword Military Classics and
Leo Cooper.

For a complete list of Pen & Sword titles please contact
PEN & SWORD BOOKS LIMITED
47 Church Street
Barnsley
South Yorkshire
S70 2AS, England
E-mail: enquiries@pen-and-sword.co.uk
Website: www.pen-and-sword.co.uk

Contents

Chapter 1	When Life was Cheap: Snitterfield, 1801	**1**
Chapter 2	The Village Moneylender: Brailes, 1808	**5**
Chapter 3	Rebecca Hodges: Ward End, 1809 and 1817	**13**
Chapter 4	A Tale of Two Forgeries: Warwickshire, 1809	**23**
Chapter 5	A Loving Family: Fillongley, 1810	**27**
Chapter 6	The Mysterious Case of the Mad Parson: Warwick, 1812	**37**
Chapter 7	The Man who was Tried Twice: Castle Bromwich and Sutton Coldfield, 1817	**41**
Chapter 8	A Robbery: Birmingham, 1825	**53**
Chapter 9	Revenge: Birmingham, 1838	**63**
Chapter 10	The Shooting: Spernall, Alcester, 1842	**69**
Chapter 11	Just Thirteen: Coventry, 1844	**76**
Chapter 12	The Poisoner: Nuneaton, 1849	**84**
Chapter 13	The Trip to Birmingham: Rugby, 1854	**90**
Chapter 14	The Brawl: Fenny Compton, 1863	**98**
Chapter 15	The Navigation Street Riot: Birmingham, 1875	**103**
Chapter 16	The Witch-Finder: Long Compton, 1875	**114**
Chapter 17	The Fortune-Teller: Birmingham, 1882 and 1883	**123**
Chapter 18	The Poisoner: Leamington Spa, 1889	**128**

Chapter 19   The Abortionist: Aston, 1895   **136**

Chapter 20   Who Killed Lucy Askham? Nuneaton,
                 1913   **145**

Chapter 21   The Belgian Asylum Seeker:
                 Birmingham, 1918   **152**

Chapter 22   The Bad Copper: Birmingham, 1928   **158**

Chapter 23   The English Penal System   **173**

Sources   **178**

Index   **179**

Acknowledgements

Thanks are due to librarians and archivists in Birmingham, Coventry, Leamington Spa, Nuneaton, Rugby, Stratford-upon-Avon and Warwick.

Map of Warwickshire showing principal locations of Foul Deeds

CHAPTER 1

When Life was Cheap

Snitterfield, 1800

On 18 November 1800, a woman's body was found in a weir break on the River Avon at Welford-on-Avon in Warwickshire, near Binton Bridge. Her throat had been cut. The body was identified as that of a Snitterfield woman, Mrs Mary Palmer, and the authorities arrested her husband John, aged twenty-six, her sister-in-law Hannah, aged nineteen, and her mother-in-law on murder charges. The mother-in-law died in gaol awaiting trial but John Palmer and Hannah Palmer were brought to trial at the Warwick Assizes on Monday 30 March 1801.

The River Avon near Binton Bridge where Mary Palmer's body was washed up. The author

It emerged that John Palmer had deserted his wife and their by this time four-year-old child several times. After the 1800 harvest John Palmer had returned to his wife to take advantage of a large quantity of grain that she had gleaned. This was waste grain lying between the stubble after the main crop had been harvested that local poor people were allowed to collect. Once the grain had gone, John Palmer decided to leave his wife again.

The mother-in-law had hated her daughter-in-law and first advised and then nagged that this time her son kill his wife. Several attempts at poisoning failed against a suspicious Mary and finally her treacherous husband, mother-in-law and sister-in-law lured her into going with them, ostensibly to pick plums. John Palmer had cut his wife's throat with a skewer while his mother and sister held her arms. John Palmer was convicted of murder and Hannah Palmer of being his accomplice. They were both sentenced to death and were publicly hanged at Warwick on Wednesday 1 April 1801.

Neither of the Palmers was given a Christian burial. John's body was taken to Binton Bridge near the scene of the murder, where it was gibbeted, which meant that it was hanged in chains and left to rot; and Hannah's body was given to a Stratford-upon-Avon surgeon Dr Gamble to be dissected. The Snitterfield villagers pulled down the mother-in-law's house.

Looking at how contemporaries viewed this crime, *The Times'* only reference to the case was a brief note on an inside page on 6 April 1801:

> At the Warwick Assizes J. Palmer was convicted of the murder of his wife and Hannah his sister of assisting in the offence and were both sentenced to die.

In 1801, Warwickshire's only local newspapers were the *Birmingham Gazette* and the *Coventry Mercury*. They both gave more attention to the case than did *The Times* but neither considered it a major news item. The *Birmingham Gazette* gave it 143 words and the *Coventry Mercury* 196 words.

One would think that at least people living near the murder scene would pay more attention but to quote the diary of a Stratford-upon-Avon lawyer Robert Hobbes:

> April 2 1801. Meeting of yeomanry but no exercise. Spoke to Sheldon about note. Two letters to Leo. Court for Clews and Chataway. Dined at the Bridgefoot today. Saw the body of the girl who was hanged for the Snitterfield murder in Gamble's

garden twice today. Home to tea and then at Falcon justicing.

April 3 1801. Good Friday. Saw the man go through Stratford to be gibbeted for Snitterfield murder. Very warm weather. Rode to Mr Lucy on Marshall's business. Saw him. Returned to dinner at four. After called on Mr Pritchard. Home to tea and walk after and then to Green Dragon to Bread Committee meeting but home to supper.

The Bread Committee was a charity which doled out bread to the very poor. Robert Hobbes was a noted local philanthropist, a volunteer charity worker or do-gooder.

Another Stratford-upon-Avon diarist, barber and wigmakers Joseph Hill, also made some brief comments about the case.

The above mentioned newspaper accounts together with the few remarks that Robert Hobbes and Joseph Hill made in their diaries, and possibly a few other scraps of information, are all the details that survive about a murder which, if it happened today, would receive massive publicity. Some may argue that the modern media, particularly the tabloids, pay far too much attention to murders. However, even the tabloids' morbid preoccupation with

Snitterfield Church where William Shakespeare's father was christened.
The author

violent death is preferable to the apparently callous lack of interest that was shown by Robert Hobbes and his contemporaries.

It is easy to criticise such an attitude towards human life but before one condemns the people of 1801, one should consider why they apparently regarded life so cheaply. Average life expectancy was just twenty-nine, meaning that half the population died before reaching that age. Even for the rich and young death was a constant companion while for the poor life was 'nasty, brutish and short.' Of course, there were people who lived into their eighties and nineties but they attracted as much attention as do centenarians today.

John and Hannah Palmer were brutal murderers and one must judge the Georgian age by its own standards, not by those of the twenty-first century when life expectancy has risen to seventy five. Snitterfield today is a charming mid-Warwickshire village. Its medieval parish church is much the same as it was in 1801. In its beautiful fourteenth century font the playwright William Shakespeare's father, John, and his uncle, Henry, were christened.

Chapter 2

The Village Moneylender

Brailes, 1808

Brailes is a south Warwickshire village. In 1808, one inhabitant was a fifty-year-old widow, Ann Newman.

Despite being on parish poor relief, which was paid for by her Northamptonshire birth parish of Aston in the Walls, Ann Newman was a moneylender. Among those she had made loans to was her twenty-four-year-old nephew by marriage, David Gardner, who lived in the same house, who was married with three children, and who had borrowed ten shillings (c. £50 in modern money); and a married couple, William and Mary Field who lived nearby, who had a twelve-year-old daughter, Ann, and who had borrowed £2 (c.£200 today). Ann Newman had found them reluctant to repay her and had repeatedly demanded her money back.

Ann Newman was last seen alive on the evening of Sunday 11 September 1808. The next day her brother, Thomas Waring, who lived nearby, in Brailes, became rather concerned but at first he thought that his sister had gone to her birth parish of Aston in the Walls. Eventually, on Thursday 15 September he visited that village to find that she was not there.

On Friday 16 September 1808, Thomas Waring and fellow Brailes villager Richard Gregory decided to search the local Brailes streams in case Ann Newman had drowned. After first unsuccessfully searching Knewt Pool they searched Sutton Brook which was about a hundred yards from her home. After dragging two deep pools they discovered Ann Newman's dead body. Her head and shoulders were lying in the brook though one leg was caught in brambles. She was partially clothed and was just wearing a gown, her head was injured and bloodstained, and blood flowed from her mouth when her body was first moved.

On Saturday 17 September, William Horniblow, a Shipston on Stour surgeon, examined the body. He found that the victim had died from a skull fracture caused by a heavy blow on the right of the head.

Suspicion fell on David Gardner. Fresh footprints had been

found near the murder scene and these were compared with one of Gardner's shoes. They matched.

David Gardner made a full confession to the murder and implicated Mary Field. He said that he and Field had been planning the murder since Christmas 1807. Mary Field first obtained some mercury, despite considerable suspicion from various shopkeepers. She then allegedly baked a cake and put mercury in it but Ann Newman found that the cake tasted odd and refused to eat anymore. Mrs Field then allegedly put some mercury in a cup of tea and gave it to her husband but he found it bitter and refused to drink any more.

Some time later Gardner and Mary Field were out chopping wood when Ann Newman passed by. Mary Field allegedly suggested killing her but Gardner refused to and his female companion accused him of faint heartedness.

Eventually, on the day of the murder, according to Gardner's confession, Gardner and Field followed the victim until she was by the brook. David Gardner hit her over the head with a hedge stake and Field strangled her with the victim's own cravat. They then cut off her pockets and took other items of clothing and having returned to the Fields' house they divided their loot. David Gardner took three half guineas and four seven shilling pieces and Field half a guinea less in return for Gardner giving her a coat of his. They then burned their victim's pockets, her purse and her hat and the hedge stake.

Both David Gardner and Mary Field were charged with murder. A coroner's inquest returned a verdict that they had murdered the victim and they were brought to trial before the Honourable Sir John Bayley at the Warwick Lent Assizes on Monday 3 April 1809.

The prosecution case was opened by the prosecution counsel, Mr Clarke. He outlined the facts of the case, describing the victim's money lending as 'various acts of kindness'.

The first prosecution witness was Thomas Waring who described his search for his sister and the finding of her body. He explained that on the evening of the day of the murder he had been at Whichford Wakes, a festival in a nearby village, and that it had been the next day when he first noticed her missing. Richard Gregory corroborated his evidence.

The third witness was Phyllis Parker, a lodger in the same house as David Gardner, his family, and the victim. She testified that Ann Newman left home for the last time at eight in the evening on the night of the murder, saying that she was going to visit her brother, Thomas Waring. Before she left, she asked

Gardner if he would be going 'down town' but he had told her that he would be eating first. However, after Ann Newman left her house for the last time Gardner followed her out.

On the murder day Gardner had been picking damsons. He had got very worried when he lost sixpence, an amount worth perhaps £2 in modern money. David Gardner and his sister, whose name was not mentioned in the trial accounts, looked for it and he was very relieved to find it, saying that it was all the money he had.

The witness said that she had seen Gardner visiting the Fields' house. David Gardner had stood at the door talking. The witness denied having seen the two prisoners together on the day of the murder but said that on the Thursday after the murder Mary Field had come to the Gardners' house to ask David Gardner to give her some tobacco for William Field's toothache. David Gardner had not apparently complied with this request but the two prisoners had left the house together.

Once Phyllis Parker had testified the judge asked if she had seen Ann Newman lend the male prisoner any money. She replied that she had only actually seen the victim lend the male prisoner a

The *George Inn* at Lower Brailes. The author

shilling but had often heard the victim ask for the money she was owed and that on the day of the murder Gardner had paid her ten shillings.

The next witness was Mary Alexander, another Brailes resident. She said that on the Tuesday after the murder Gardner asked her to change two shillings for him as they were 'too pretty' to have to spend. She gave him another shilling for one and change for the other. One of the shillings was dated 1711 and had two heads on it and in response to sharp questions from the judge she said that she would know these shillings if she saw them again.

Thomas Richardson, the Acting Village Constable of Brailes, then gave evidence. He said that Mary Alexander had brought the two shillings to him at the *George Inn* in Brailes after the news of the murder. He had passed them onto the coroner who eventually returned them to Richardson who produced them in court. Neither of them had two heads on and perhaps the coins had got mixed up by mistake.

The sixth witness was Sarah Calloway, a Shipston on Stour publican. She said that on either the Tuesday or the Wednesday after the murder, Gardner had come into her pub and bought a quart of ale to drink in, and two quarts to take out. He took the money out of a 'linen rag'.

Edward Weeks, a Brailes shopkeeper, was then called. He said that on the Tuesday after the murder the female prisoner had changed a five shilling piece in his shop in payment for flour.

Ann Newman's sister, Frances Hobbins, gave evidence. She told the court that on the Thursday before the murder she had seen the victim empty her purse upon the table. It contained either three or four half guineas, several seven shilling pieces, a five shilling piece and several 'pretty' shillings.

Thomas Richardson then gave evidence again, saying that on the Friday after the body was found he searched the female prisoner's house and found some clothes which had belonged to Ann Newman there.

The ninth witness was John Hyde. He and Thomas Clifton had arrested Gardner after the body was found. David Gardner who had been 'loading beans on Mr Wright's ground' came willingly with Hyde and Clifton to the George Inn's kitchen where they and several other people accused him of murder. The male prisoner at first denied murder but after a while asked Hyde if they could go into the pub garden with them for a private talk.

The male prisoner asked Hyde what he had 'better do in this job.' The witness asked: 'What job?' and Gardner replied: 'About my Aunt' (i.e. the victim).

The judge interjected, asking if Gardner had been made any promises. The witness explained that Gardner had asked if he would get off if he was the first to confess, to be told that he would have the best chance.

As Gardner was about to confess Hyde realised the need for a witness to the confession and fetched Acting Parish Constable Richardson. John Hyde asked Richardson if Gardner would get off if he was the first to confess and Richardson also told him that he would have the best chance. David Gardner then named Mary Field as his accomplice.

David Gardner had left home on the evening of the murder, telling his wife and Phyllis Parker that he was going to meet his father coming home from Whichford Wake. He went towards his father's but as he passed the Fields's house Mary Field called him in and asked him to go with her to Thomas Willis's to get some plums or apples. As they went out the female prisoner asked Gardner to take a hedge stake with him which he did. Once the two prisoners were safely out of the house Mary Field suggested that she and Gardner should 'do for your aunt today'. David Gardner reluctantly agreed and they committed the murder as described above.

After this confession Gardner showed Hyde, Thomas Clifton and Thomas Buckinghamshire, the murder scene. Once Hyde had testified Thomas Clifton corroborated his evidence. The male prisoner interrupted the court proceedings and said that Hyde and Clifton had shown him the murder scene rather than the other way round but predictably they denied this.

Thomas Richardson was recalled to the witness box for a third time. He corroborated Hyde's evidence and told the court that after Gardner's confession he and two other men arrested Mary Field. At first she denied the murder charge but when she had been taken to the *George* Richardson had told her of Gardner's confession. Mary Field then said that as Gardner had 'squeaked' she would too. She said that she had left her home with Gardner to go to Willis's to get some plums and that Gardner had killed the victim with his stick. Mary Field denied murder but admitted to having helped rob the victim.

The witness then asked the female prisoner what had happened to the items she had stolen from the victim to be told that she had wrapped her share of the stolen money in a black handkerchief and placed it in a cupboard. Acting Constable Richardson then sent John Taplin to search the Fields' house. He was accompanied by the Fields' daughter who had accompanied her mother when she was arrested. John Taplin found the handkerchief, which contained three half guineas, two seven shilling pieces and two silver shillings.

John Taplin then corroborated Acting Constable Richardson's evidence. He also said that he had asked Gardner what motive he had for the murder, to be told that it was for the sake of his aunt's money.

Richard Richardson, the Brailes schoolmaster, was the eleventh witness. He had taken down David Gardner's confession in writing and had read it back to him to check its accuracy. The Clerk of the Court then read it to the court.

Two more witnesses, William Carter of Epwell and John Millward, then helped to corroborate the above evidence. James Brown, a Brailes man, then testified that after Gardner's arrest but before Mary Field's arrest he had told her about Gardner's arrest. Mary Field had told him that she would be able to give Gardner a good alibi.

The fifteenth witness was William Horniblow, the Shipston on Stour surgeon who had examined the victim's body. He described her injuries and in response to a question by the judge said that the wounds tallied with Gardner's confession. This evidence was corroborated by Amos Middleton, a Warwick surgeon, and John Dove, a Shipston on Stour surgeon.

The prosecution had made its case. The prisoners were asked if they wished to say anything in their own defence. Mary Field declined to say anything. David Gardner admitted his involvement but said that he had been drunk and that he had intended robbery rather than murder, and that Mary Field had instigated the attack.

The judge summed up, first warning the jury that if either prisoner were convicted of murder they would hang. He went over the evidence in detail. Having done so he explained that Gardner's confession was properly made and had been thoroughly corroborated. However, although it was very strong evidence against Gardner it was not acceptable evidence against Field. Her own confession was not acceptable either as she had said that Gardner had killed the victim and that she had merely helped to rob the victim, having initially gone out with Gardner for what she thought was a lawful purpose, i.e. picking plums.

After deliberating for a quarter of an hour the jury convicted David Gardner of murder and acquitted Mary Field. The judge then sentenced Gardner to death, saying that regardless of who had instigated the murder, it was a 'transgression equally offensive to the laws of God and Man' for the condemned man had murdered an aunt who had been kind to him.

Lower Brailes Church. The author

The jury then told the judge that although their verdict was unanimous, they were concerned in case Mary Field escape justice. The judge agreed and said that the female prisoner would be detained until the next Assize, when she would be tried as an accessory to the murder after the fact.

After the trial, David Gardner admitted his guilt but continued to insist that Mary Field had instigated the murder. David Gardner was hanged outside Warwick Gaol on Wednesday 5 April 1809, two days after the trial. In his last speech to the public he admitted his crime, said that he hoped that God would forgive him and that he hoped to go to heaven. He warned the spectators to heed his fate and avoid temptation.

Mary Field was brought to trial again at the Warwick Summer Assizes on Thursday 3 August 1809. The prosecution evidence against her was basically the same as that at the earlier trial. In addition, the prosecution called her twelve-year-old daughter as a witness and asked her, under oath, where her mother had been at the time of the murder. The judge, Sir Simon Le Blanc, ruled this question out of order.

Also, some clothes of Ann Newman's had been found in Mary

Field's house and were produced in court but the judge said that this evidence did not relate to the charge of being an accessory after the fact, which meant that someone had helped to conceal the perpetrator of a murder after the attack.

After the prosecution evidence, the judge told the jury to acquit Mary Field which they did. The judge at the first trial should have had her charged with theft of which she was clearly guilty and which would have led to her being transported to Australia. She had not escaped all punishment, as she had spent eleven months in an early nineteenth century gaol. She presumably then returned home and one wonders what sort of a reception she got from her husband who she had allegedly attempted to poison!

Was Mary Field an adulteress and village Lady Macbeth or was she a desperate and poverty-stricken housewife who had panicked under stress? I leave it to the reader to decide.

Brailes is still an attractive village. Its magnificent medieval Anglican parish church is one of the largest in south Warwickshire. It also houses a small Roman Catholic chapel which was built in 1726 and is attached to the seventeenth century manor house. The chapel is one of the oldest places of Catholic worship in England, built when Roman Catholicism was still officially illegal though a blind eye was usually turned to Catholic gentry families whose religious faith was willing to endure the institutionalised discrimination which Catholics faced.

CHAPTER 3

Rebecca Hodges

Ward End, 1809 and 1817

My first book *The Trials of Rebecca* was self-published in 1987, in the far off days when Margaret Thatcher was Prime Minister, Ronald Reagan American President and Mikhaill Gorbachev the Soviet leader. It described the case of Rebecca Hodges, who was tried first for attempted murder and then for arson in the early nineteenth century. This book was mainly circulated inside the Birmingham area and is long out of print and new information has now emerged from Australia about Rebecca's life.

Rebecca Hodges was born in 1780. A description of her in adulthood describes her as five foot three inches tall, with a ruddy complexion, grey eyes and dark brown hair. In December 1801 she got a job working for Samuel Birch, a farmer of Ward End Hall, Ward End, near Birmingham. She and her supporters claimed that she became the farmer's mistress before losing his favour and was sacked in August 1802 after having gone to fetch a pail of water on a Saturday, only returning on the Monday.

Rebecca brooded over her wrongs and at eleven in the evening on 27 February 1809 she entered Samuel Birch's farmhouse kitchen. As he slept she shot him twice in the head with a pistol she had bought from a Mr Phillips on the pretext that she wanted it for protection against burglars. Fortunately for both Rebecca and her victim Samuel Birch survived after a trepanation. One bullet grazed his scalp and the other lodged between his scalp and his skull.

At three in the morning on 28 February 1809, Hodges was arrested by a Birmingham watchman, John Wood, in Dale End on the Ward End side of Birmingham. She was wearing men's clothing consisting of a dark coat, waistcoat, trousers and a round hat and he at first thought that she was a man. He found a cocked pistol under her arm and handed her over to William Payn, the keeper of Birmingham Gaol.

Miss Hodges was brought to trial at the Warwickshire Lent Assizes on Monday 3 April 1809. Nine witnesses testified. They

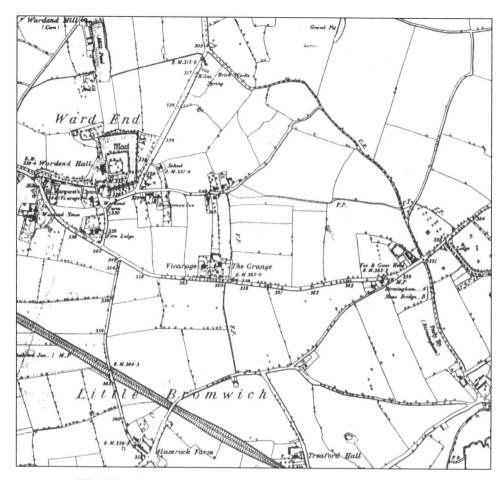

Ward End, from the 6 inch to 1 mile OS map of 1887. Ordnance Survey

were Samuel Birch; his niece and housekeeper Sarah Bradbury; his servant Thomas Hammond; Mr Vickers, the surgeon who had treated the victim; John Wood and William Payn; Mary Taylor, who had sold Hodges men's clothing a year before; Mr Phillips who had sold her the gun, and Richard Gaillimore, a boy who lived at Saltley Turnpike Gate, the historic Saltley Gates and who had been questioned by Hodges about her victim's movements.

Five witnesses appeared for the defence arguing that Rebecca was insane. Francis Woodcock, a Worcestershire magistrate, with whom Hodges had lodged and worked for three years before she worked for Samuel Birch, said that she had habitually talked to herself, had gone absent without permission, danced by herself in the fields and wandered about picking up sticks and putting them down again. Mr Woodcock's servant, Lawrence Townley, corroborated his master's evidence.

Mary Tupper, the defendant's married sister, said that Rebecca would go walking shoeless for miles, would go out nearly naked and had in 1799, when still a teenager, tried to hang herself. The prisoner's father, William Hodges, supported his daughter's evidence and finally William Walker, a servant of Samuel Birch, described her as being 'flighty' and as having repeatedly threatened to drown herself on being teased by her fellow workers.

The judge, Sir John Bayley, summed up, recommending that the jury acquit the prisoner as insane. The jury agreed and Rebecca spent the next seven years in Warwick Gaol and then a year at the New Saint Bethlehem Lunatic Asylum in London, also known as Bedlam. In August 1817, after repeated letters appealing to her victim for mercy she was released from Bedlam as having recovered her sanity.

Rebecca returned to Birmingham and on Sunday 14 December 1817 she was arrested and charged with arson having allegedly set fire to and partially destroyed one of Samuel Birch's haystacks and two of his wheat stacks at three in the morning on Friday 12 December. She was brought to trial at the Warwick Lent Assizes on Saturday 4 April 1818. The judge was the Honourable Sir William Garrow and the prosecution counsel were Messrs Reader and Reynolds. Rebecca defended herself.

The prosecution produced twenty witnesses. Samuel Birch described the accused's previous history and he, his wagon driver, Mr Houghton, and his cowman, Thomas Williams, described the fire, which had been started in several places around the bottom of the stacks. This showed that they were the result of arson rather than spontaneous combustion.

Rebecca Hodges' landlady, Catherine Mason, a widow with five children, testified that Rebecca had been absent from her lodgings on the night of the fire. George Hemmings, the landlord of *The Swan* in Ashted on the Ward End side of Birmingham, said that Hodges had been in his pub from half ten to eleven at night on Thursday 11 December 1817. She had been wearing a dark cloth coat, a black bonnet and had a spotted handkerchief tied around her neck.

A Washwood Heath farmer, William Blizzard, and his son Joseph, had been up on the morning of the fire because the son was going to Dudley with a load of flour. The son asked a passing woman, who was wearing a long dark coat and a black bonnet and who was going towards Birmingham, if she knew what the fire was. The woman answered: 'No.'

A Washwood Heath girl, Mary Perry, testified to having found a piece of woman's half-neck handkerchief, a form of cravat which was coloured with purple and white spots, near one of the burnt haystacks. She gave it to her thimble-maker mother, Jane Perry, who gave it to a Ward End farmer's wife, Mrs Phoebe Briscoe, who passed it on to a Joseph Lovell, a Birmingham man who gave it to William Payn, the High Constable of Birmingham. The latter testified that the handkerchief piece matched another piece that had been found in a bundle of material when Rebecca was arrested; and that a dark-coloured woman's cloak had also been found in her possession.

John Boucher, a Birmingham linen draper, gave the court his expert opinion that the two pieces of handkerchief came from the same handkerchief, matching in every detail of colour, pattern and fabric.

William Bulloes, a Castle Bromwich bricklayer, had been walking between Washwood Heath and Aston on the morning of the fire. The road he used is today Aston Church Road and Holborn Hill. On the road Bulloes found a tinderbox with a piece of a rag inside it, and an old checked pocket handkerchief with a bottle of phosphorous and some matches wrapped in it. He gave these items to William Payn in the same state as he found them. The piece of rag was of the same pattern as a gown and some small pieces of printed cotton which had been found in the prisoner's bundle.

Samuel Evans, who lived in Birmingham's London Prentice Street, testified that in August 1817 the accused had visited his house because she and his wife were old friends. Rebecca had allegedly threatened revenge on Samuel Birch, saying: 'I'll be damned if I don't kill him or burn his house down.'

Susannah Milner, of Snow Hill, Birmingham, then a residential area, told the court that she had known the prisoner in Warwick Gaol when they were fellow inmates. Six weeks before the fire Hodges had visited her and said: 'Revenge is sweet. I shall either blow his brains out or set his ricks on fire.'

Rebecca Hodges had cross examined many of the witnesses but her questioning had mainly been futile. However, she successfully discredited Evans and Milner. Samuel Evan's wife had a conviction for keeping a 'disorderly house' and Susannah Milner was a notorious brothel keeper.

William Payn, the High Constable of Birmingham, and George

Redfern, an Assistant Constable of Birmingham, described the contradictory alibis that the prisoner had allegedly given them. One turned out to relate to events on a night previous to the fire as was confirmed by a Birmingham watchman Joseph Bedworth, who described how on the night of Thursday 4 December he had helped a drunk Rebecca Hodges to her lodgings and knocked on the door for her to no avail.

George Wallet of the Medical Department of the Bethlehem Hospital in London (Bedlam) and Henry Tatnall, the keeper of Warwick Gaol, testified that in their opinion the prisoner was completely sane. This was despite having spent seven years in an early nineteenth century prison and a year in an early nineteenth century lunatic asylum which would have driven many sane people mad. Her previous strange behaviour as described at the earlier trial must have been at most the actions of a confused teenager.

Once the prosecution had made its case, Rebecca spoke in her own defence, saying that she left her lodgings on Thursday 11 December at four in the afternoon, planning to see her aunt in Deritend. On her way she met an old friend, Hannah, who had got married, becoming Mrs Hannah Webster. They shared three pints of ale in a Dudley Street pub and Rebecca agreed to help Hannah carry a load part of the way to Halesowen but explained that she could not go all the way as she had to go to Footherley to visit her sister and brother-in-law and collect some money that he owed her.

Rebecca said that she accompanied her friend Hannah Webster for four miles along the Halesowen road and then returned. When she got back to her lodgings, she continuously knocked on the door but received no answer. A man who looked like a gentleman's coachman came and asked her what was the matter and she told him that she was locked out of her lodgings.

After realising that she was locked out Rebecca went up another street where she heard a row and a woman saying: '. . . you'll send your master a bag of malt tomorrow morning you may depend on it.' Rebecca entered the house where she had heard this conversation not realising that it was a pub and found a drunk woman and a ostler. The woman said that she would go and Rebecca asked the ostler who the woman was. She was told that the ostler knew the drunk woman very well and again made remarks that the editor of the *Warwick Advertiser* declined to print. Rebecca expressed concern for the woman's safety as she could hardly stand up.

Another person in the pub asked if the drunk woman was 'Betty Blue' (a nickname) and the ostler said it was and asked the other person what he thought of her. Rebecca left the pub, as did a young 'chap' and at the end of the entry Rebecca heard a scuffle and the young chap said: '. . . me, if old Mother Haynes isn't turning the woman out neck and crop.' At this point the drunken woman came tumbling down the entry. Rebecca and the young man followed her and the woman entered another pub, *The Castle*.

The young man said: 'Why . . . my eyes, if she isn't gone into the Castle now what the . . . does she want to do there I'm sure she's got as much as she can carry.' Rebecca and the young man followed the drunk woman into *The Castle*'s kitchen and saw her sitting by the fireside. Rebecca and the young man ordered half a pint of ale each. The drunk woman said: '. . . me, I've got no money to buy any ale'. Another customer let her share his pint.

The drunk woman started singing and laughing and the landlord came to turn her out to be told: '. . . I'll have your sign pulled down you villain I will.' Another woman said that the drunken woman's name was Mary Blower, also known as 'Betty Blue'.

The drunken woman left the pub saying that she would go to Brownell. Rebecca followed her for a while but lost track of her near Birmingham Barracks. Rebecca then went into a pub and had another half pint of ale. There were two young men, an old woman and a cat in the pub.

After this drink, Rebecca went down Aston Street and sat down and cried at being locked out of her lodgings and being on the street that late at night. A man came to her and asked if she had lost her husband. She told him that her landlady had locked her out and he warned her that she was risking a vagrancy charge. The man tried to find some lodgings for her but failed and they went down a dark narrow entry and found an outside privy where they slept from midnight to five in the morning. When her companion left he gave her a shilling.

Rebecca Hodges told the court that she then went to her sister's at Footherley on the day after the night of the fire, by way of Aston Park Wall (i.e., past Aston Hall). She collected the money her sister owed her and on Saturday 13 December she set off home, reaching the *Bluebell Tavern* (whose landlady was related to her) at half past ten in the morning and, had two pints of ale and some food. She then passed through Sutton Coldfield where she stopped for another drink and then returned to her

Birmingham lodgings where she gave her landlady's daughter a shilling that she owed the landlady and went to bed. She was arrested the next day.

The prisoner told the court that she was as innocent as a newborn child. While she had been imprisoned awaiting trial she had been denied visitors and no one had been allowed to speak to her.

The judge then summed up. He admitted that all the evidence was circumstantial but said that it was necessary to use such evidence because in such a crime as arson, which carried the death penalty, no sane person would confess or employ an accomplice who might turn King's Evidence.

Rebecca Hodges had a clear motive. She had been absent from her lodgings on the night of the arson, she had been seen in a pub between her lodgings and the scene of the fire late in the evening before it. A person resembling her was seen leaving the area where the fires had happened, and there was strong forensic evidence against her i.e. the matching pieces of neck handkerchief and the matching rag from the tinderbox. The judge admitted that Samuel Evans and Susannah Milner were dubious witnesses but their story of the prisoner's threats rang true. Good evidence showed that the accused was sane.

The jury took three minutes to convict Rebecca Hodges of arson and the judge then sentenced her to death, saying that this was one of the worst arson cases he had ever come across. The prisoner was left for execution and there were widespread newspaper reports that she had been hanged.

A pamphlet about this case was produced and widely circulated with the help of subsidies from the Norwich Union Insurance Association. There was even a song which went:

Mourn, Mourn ye tender people all
Rejoice not at my sad downfall
For when I in the dust am laid
Remember Satan me betrayed

Rebecca Hodges is my name
My friends do not me blame
Revenge prompted my arm so dread
I shot my master through the head

I quickly was to prison sent
My heart too stubborn to repent
I pleaded there like one insane
And got imprisoned for the same

By chance I did not take his life
I could not hope to be his wife
Therefore when I my freedom got
My passion and revenge was hot

Straightway I went to Ward End
Like unto a wicked fiend
I set the ricks on fire that night
Because I thought he did me slight

I was found and I was taken
And brought to Warwick for the same
Where quickly I was found guilty
And doomed to suffer on a tree

I heard my sentence with surprise
The hall it echoed with my cries
"My Lord some pity take on me
And let me still imprisoned be"

No mercy to me he would show
So I must suffer here below
Take warning pray good people all
And pity my unhappy fall.

Rebecca Hodges's sentence was commuted to transportation for life. On 1 May 1819 the *Warwick Advertiser* noted that she had been removed from Warwick Gaol to sail on the *Lord Wellington* from Woolwich. She arrived in Australia on 20 January 1820.

Rebecca Hodges did various manual jobs and gave birth to two children out of wedlock in Australia. Her first son, Charles, the son of a convict, George Kenniwell, who had been transported for embezzling £60, was born in October 1821 when the baby's mother was aged forty-one. A second son, George, was born in 1823. In 1827 the forty-seven-year-old Rebecca married Thomas Wilkins, a forty-year-old fellow life transportee who worked as a farm overseer at Mulgoa and Bringelly in New South Wales.

In 1833, the now fifty-three-year-old Rebecca Wilkins nee Hodges obtained a ticket of leave and in July 1837 she was conditionally pardoned, meaning that she was free within Australia. She died of old age in 1860, aged eighty, at Camperdown Benevolent Asylum and is buried in Camperdown Cemetery.

Rebecca Hodges had certainly tried to murder her victim in 1809. She was almost certainly guilty of arson against him in

Ward End Parish Church, built in 1833, fifteen years after Rebecca Hodges was transported. Today it is Ward End's oldest building. The author

1817. An imaginative novelist might weave a story in which a personal enemy of Samuel Birch had his stacks set on fire, having lured Rebecca from her lodgings and planted evidence with the connivance of the Birmingham police. In reality, though, such a tale belongs to the realms of fantasy.

The name 'Rebecca Hodges' was to be frequently used on anonymous letters threatening arson. It was often shortened to 'Rebecca' and is a strong candidate for the origins of the name 'The Rebecca Riots' in Wales in the 1840s, when angry crowds calling themselves 'The Daughters of Rebecca' burnt the hated turnpike gates at which people had to pay tolls to use the public highways.

Ward End and Washwood Heath are today completely urbanised. Not a single building survives from 1818. St Margaret's Anglican Church in Ward End was built in 1833 on the same site as the similarly dedicated previous church. Some major roads and some pub names also survive, though the pubs themselves have been rebuilt, places which the participants in the trials would recognise. Ward End Hall was long ago demolished to make way for a Secondary Modern School called Ward End Hall, which became a comprehensive and which has itself been demolished to make way for a housing estate.

CHAPTER 4

A Tale of Two Forgeries

Warwickshire, 1809

In April 1809 police raided the house of a sixty-four-year-old Birmingham woman Susannah Grant and discovered an edger, a tool designed to mark, in this case, seven shilling pieces, round the edges. It was illegal to possess such a tool without a proper licence. The prisoner said that the tool had been left in her house by a lodger, admitted to having known that her house was being used to store forged money but denied knowing that it was being used for actual forgery.

Susannah Grant was tried at the Warwick Summer Assizes in

The front of Warwick County Gaol where prisoners were once hanged.
The author

EXECUTION OF PATRICK WICKHAM AND SUSANNAH GRANT.

Yesterday morning, about half past eleven o'clock, Patrick Wickham, convicted at the late Assize for this county, of shooting Mr. Avern in January last, on Stank-hill, near this town, and also of robbing Mr. Gardner, between this place and Longbridge turnpike, and Susannah Grant, for having in her possession, at Birmingham, an edger, or instrument for marking seven shilling pieces round the edges, were executed over the door of the county gaol.

Wickham, although a young man, had been concerned in several robberies, besides those for which he suffered. He had, since his condemnation, been penitent and resigned; and, being a Roman Catholic, he was attended by a gentleman of that persuasion, whose spiritual admonitions appeared to have had their intended influence upon his mind. He did not make any confession, publicly. When he was tied up, and just before the cap was drawn over his face, he said—" *God forgive my prosecutors, for I am innocent of what I suffer for.*"— Wickham was a serjeant in the 103d foot, and only 24 years of age.

Susannah Grant was far advanced in years, being 64 years of age. She acknowledged that she well knew that base money was concealed in her house, having let one of her rooms for that express purpose; but she positively denied having taken any part in the coining of the money, or that money was ever made in her house. With regard to the instrument that was found in her house, she appeared to have no knowledge of its being there; neither, she said, was she aware that the concealment of such an instrument in her house was a capital offence. She was penitent, firm, and collected, and confident in the hope of forgiveness. " *I pray,*" she said, " *for myself and all mankind, and hope my fate will be a warning to others.*"—She expressed her warmest gratitude to the Chaplain who attended her, and prayed incessantly. The executioner performed the last sad office, and they were both launched into eternity, in presence of a large concourse of spectators.

The execution of Patrick Wickham and Susannah Grant as shown in the *Warwick Advertiser*, 19 August 1809. Birmingham Library

August 1809 and was sentenced to death. She was hanged in front of Warwick Gaol on Friday 18 August 1809, alongside Sergeant Patrick Wickham of the 103rd Regiment (later the 2nd Royal Dublin Fusiliers) who had been convicted of attempted murder and armed robbery.

At the same assizes there was another notable forgery trial. To quote the *Birmingham Gazette* of Monday 7 August 1809:

At these assizes a very important case as far as respects the banking and commercial interests of this country came on to be tried. The prisoners, Thomas Charles Fitzhugh Sandon, and William Hitchen, two well known characters and part of a very numerous gang of swindlers, who have long been in the habit of defrauding the public by opening fictitious banks, were charged with having conspired with Joseph Bullock (who had assumed the name of Joseph Albert Bullock) John Horner, Robert Kennett, and William Peter Joggett, to defraud the public, by opening a bank at Southampton under the style of the Southampton and Hampshire Bank; and under the firm of Joseph Albert Bullock, John Horner and Co., and uttering divers five pound and other notes and drafts of that bank, particularly in the County of Warwick and in the City of Coventry, and thereby obtaining money and goods to a very considerable extent.

It appeared in evidence that the parties composing the above nefarious bank were men in abject poverty and desperate circumstances, and that the bank was opened merely to give a colour and pretext for the issuing of the notes and save the parties from the consequences of a capital offence. After a trial of seven hours and the examination of a great number of witnesses the prisoners were convicted of the offence charged in the indictment, to the satisfaction of a very crowded court. The learned judge, Sir Simon Le Blanc, in a most forcible and impressive address to the prisoners, pointed out to them the enormity of the offence, and the great injury it was calculated to do by destroying the confidence of the people in regard to that necessary circulating medium, the paper currency of the country, and that the parties to so great and glaring a fraud might be held up to public ignominy, and their persons well known, sentenced the prisoners to twelve months imprisonment in the House of Correction and to stand in the pillory on some market day in the town of Warwick.

Counsel for the prosecution were Mr Clarke, Mr Davrell and Mr Reader; with solicitors Messrs Inge and Carter Coventry and Mr Whateley Birmingham. Counsel for the prisoners were Mr Serjeant Vaughan and Mr Reynolds; and solicitor Mr Earl, Kenilworth.

In other words, letting forgers use one's house could mean death. Meanwhile, grandiosely setting up a fake bank meant a year in prison and a spell in the pillory. The pillory was a wooden framework into which prisoners were locked by the head and wrists and exposed to public hostility such as the throwing of rotten eggs.

The judge in these two trials was, as quoted, Sir Simon Le Blanc (1749–1816). A descendant of Huguenot refugees, he was well known for his strict sentences, though he had shown mercy to the alleged Brailes murderess Mary Field (Chapter 2). His frustration at the weakness of a criminal law that tied his hands behind his back when dealing with swindlers who grandiosely set up a fake bank, rather than merely printing false money, was doubtless why he sentenced Sandon and Hitchen to be pilloried as well as to be gaoled. It may also have helped inspire his savage treatment of Susannah Grant.

CHAPTER 5

A Loving Family

Fillongley, 1810

On 27 January 1810 the *Warwick Advertiser* reported that John Danks, a forty-two-year-old farm labourer from Fillongley, a Warwickshire village eight miles north of Coventry, had been charged by a coroner's inquest with murdering his newborn illegitimate grandchild. Also, John Danks' eighteen-year-old daughter, Hannah Danks, whose child it was, and her twenty-three-year-old half-brother, Edward Grooby, had been charged with being accomplices to the murder.

John and Hannah Danks and Edward Grooby were brought for trial before the Honourable Sir John Bayley at the Warwick Lent Assizes on 4 April 1810. After the indictment against the three

Fillongley village today. The author

Fillongley's medieval church. The author

prisoners had been read to the court, the prosecution opened the case by calling the first witness, a Fillongley woman called Ann Barr who lived in the house next-door-but-one to the Danks's home.

Ann Barr explained that she knew all of John Danks's family, who were John Danks, his wife Sarah, their daughter Hannah, Edward Grooby, who was Sarah Danks's son by another man, and a boy of eleven. The trial transcripts fail to mention whether Grooby was Sarah Danks's child by an earlier marriage, whether he was born out of wedlock before she got married or whether she had had an affair with another man during her marriage. Ann Barr said that she had known that Hannah Danks was pregnant and that the father of her unborn child was Grooby, her half-brother.

Having described the background to the pregnancy, which would have created a far worse scandal than would have followed an ordinary pregnancy out of wedlock, Ann Barr said that she had been at the Danks's house on 15 January 1810 together with another neighbour, Hannah Proctor, who was also in court. Ann Barr and Hannah Proctor had delivered Hannah Danks's baby in the kitchen. They had then taken Hannah Danks upstairs and put her to bed, in a room with three beds in it. Soon after, they took the baby upstairs and put it to bed with its mother. The two women then left and went home at ten in the evening.

At about three the next morning John Danks called round and told Ann Barr that his grandchild was dead. Ann Barr returned to the Danks's house and found the baby lying dead in a kitchen armchair.

The witness asked John Danks if he had been to bed. He said that he had but had had to get up because his toes were too cold for him to sleep – a common enough feeling in an unheated bedroom in January! Shortly after he got up he heard his daughter call for her mother to carry the baby downstairs. John Danks told Ann Barr that he had met his wife as she was carrying the baby downstairs and took it off her. He then took the baby into the kitchen and looked at it closely. He realised it was dead and went for help.

Having described her conversation with John Danks, the witness told the court that the child appeared to be quite normal at birth and concluded by saying that she had not had any conversation with Grooby about the baby.

On being cross-examined by the defence counsel, Ann Barr said that when she had dressed the child before she put it to bed she had accidentally put its feet in the armholes. She denied having said that the baby would probably die.

The second witness was Hannah Proctor, John Danks's next door neighbour. She said that Hannah Danks had actually been delivered of her baby on the witness's lap in the kitchen, and that Ann Barr and herself had taken the baby upstairs. Next, the two women had dressed the baby in a shirt and cap borrowed from local woman, Deborah Page, as the mother herself had only prepared 'a yard of flannel'. The child had seemed healthy.

The witness said to Edward Grooby: 'You must take care of this woman and child; 'tis so much like you'. Grooby had smiled at this remark.

Hannah Proctor then went home but returned in time to help Ann Barr take the baby up to bed. It still seemed healthy. Hannah Danks was in one bed and Edward Grooby was sleeping in another bed in the same room. The two women had laid the child on its mother's left arm.

The next morning, Hannah Proctor heard that the baby was dead. She had helped to put its body into a small wooden coffin and said that she failed to spot any evident cause of death. John Danks told her the same story about what had happened the previous night, that he had told Ann Barr.

From the above evidence, the Danks clearly lived in a two-bedroom cottage. John Danks and his wife slept in one bedroom and Hannah Danks, Edward Grooby, and the young boy whose relationship to the rest of the household is not mentioned in the trial accounts, slept in the other one.

The third witness was Patrick Simpson, a Fillongley surgeon. He said that he was called to the Danks's house on Thursday 18 January 1810, to examine the baby's body. It had been placed in a nailed-down wooden coffin but he had the coffin opened up.

Surgeon Simpson examined the body and noticed serious bruising on both sides of the throat which looked as if they had been made by the pressure of hands. This suggested that the baby had been strangled and he reported this to the coroner who organised an inquest.

Because of the coming inquest Simpson dissected the baby's corpse on Saturday 20 January. He said that the 'turgid' appearance of the brain further suggested that the baby had been strangled, and said that the local clergyman had been there when he dissected the body of the baby, which was a boy. He denied that the birth was premature.

On cross-examination by the defence, Simpson admitted that he had been asked to deliver the baby but had refused to do so because of other commitments that day. He also denied that that baby's injuries might have been caused by Ann Barr and Hannah Proctor being clumsy when they dressed the baby.

The judge then questioned Simpson, first asking how long the pressure that had caused such marks would have taken to kill the baby. Simpson replied that it would have taken about a quarter of an hour. The judge asked if two minutes of such pressure would have been fatal and Simpson denied this but admitted that five minutes might have been fatal, especially if the baby had been in a weak state. A newborn baby would, he admitted, have been very vulnerable.

Having established that it would take some time to strangle a baby and only produce bruising, the judge asked Simpson if the baby's struggles might have been so weak that someone sleeping in the same bed might be able to sleep through it. Surgeon Simpson said that this was improbable but in response to further questions by the judge admitted that women often sleep very heavily after giving birth.

After Simpson had testified Hannah Proctor was recalled. After

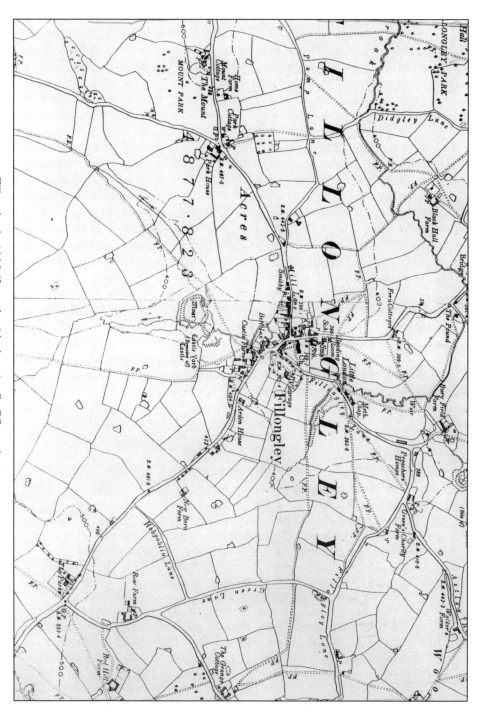

Fillongley in 1905 (from the 6 inch to 1 mile OS map). Ordnance Survey

saying that Simpson had been summoned to the delivery but had been unable to come, she explained that she had persuaded Edward Grooby to fetch a doctor to look at the baby's body by warning that if he failed to do this he would end up 'with a halter round your neck'. She then explained that it had been Grooby who had told her that his half-sister was pregnant. Hannah Proctor said that Hannah Danks had had a relatively easy time in childbirth despite it being her first pregnancy, and concluded by saying that she had known her since childhood and so knew for sure that this was her first pregnancy.

The fourth witness was Coventry surgeon John Smith-Soden. He said that he had seen the baby's corpse on Monday 22 January, two days after Patrick Simpson had opened it up. He corroborated his colleague's evidence and testified that he too believed that the baby had been strangled.

In cross examination Smith-Soden said that it would have taken some two to three minutes to strangle a baby and only leave bruises such as those that he and Simpson had seen on its neck. He denied that such marks could have been caused by a baby being smothered by the bedclothes or that a wind attack could have suffocated it and left such marks. However, he admitted that women who had recently given birth were prone to making sudden involuntary movements in their sleep. In response to a question by the judge, he accepted that women often sleep very heavily after giving birth.

The next witness was Charles Woodcock, the son of the coroner at the inquest. No reason was given for his father's absence at the trial. He read out a confession that Grooby had made at the inquest. It read:

Hannah Danks was put to bed on the Monday night; she saw the child in the kitchen; between twelve and one John Danks went upstairs and got into bed. In a quarter of an hour afterwards he saw John Danks get up, go to the child and with his right hand squeeze him by the throat; he heard the child cry out; and then John Danks got into bed again. At five o'clock he saw the child lie in the kitchen; Grooby asked Hannah Danks how she did and she said she was very sorry the child was dead.

Charles Woodcock explained that Hannah Danks had told the coroner that she had done nothing to hurt the child and had not seen anyone else do so. She had, she said, woken up and found the baby dead. She had seen her father going downstairs and called to him to fetch her mother. Hannah Danks was distressed and her father had told her not to cry.

The prosecution case then closed. The three prisoners had clearly all got a very strong motive for murder i.e. removing the living witness of behaviour that would cause a major scandal today, let alone in 1810. The baby had clearly been strangled and Grooby had confessed to having seen John Danks do the murder and had done nothing to try and stop him.

The defence case was opened by Hannah Danks who stated that she had '. . . never injured the child nor anybody else that I know of.. Edward Grooby retracted his earlier confession to the coroner and said: 'I never saw anybody injure it to my knowledge; I never injured it, nor anybody else that I know of.' The defence called no witnesses.

Once the defence had closed, the judge recalled Ann Barr to the witness box. In reply to his questions she stated that when she had laid the baby on its mother's left arm she had asked her to take good care of it and warned her not to let 'the clothes lie on its mouth and its nose.' Hannah Danks had replied: 'God bless it, neighbour, I will not hurt it.'

The judge, Sir John Bayley, then made his closing speech to the jury. He reminded them that the three accused were indicted for the murder of a male illegitimate child, of which Hannah Danks was the mother and her half-brother Edward Grooby the father. He said that the jury had to decide three questions. Firstly, was the child killed by the 'violence spoken of?' Secondly, were all the three prisoners 'guilty as charged'. Thirdly, and finally, if the jury did not think that they all were guilty, then which if any of them were actually guilty?

Having explained what the jury must do the judge said that in his opinion the medical evidence was unclear, and reminded them that it had been a week after the death before a proper post-mortem was done. The judge thought that Simpson's theory that it might take anything up to a quarter of an hour to strangle a baby was rather strange. However, he admitted that both surgeons who had testified thought that the baby had been strangled but said that the jury still had to decide which, if any of the three prisoners were responsible.

There was very little evidence against Hannah Danks and there were points in her favour. She had not tried to keep her pregnancy secret from her neighbours and she had reportedly seemed distressed at the death of her child. The judge said that even if the child had been murdered, its mother might simply have been fast asleep at the time. Neither was there any evidence strong enough to convict John Danks. Edward Grooby's confession was valid evidence against Grooby but was unsupported and so was not valid against John Danks. The judge pointed out that John Danks had quickly fetched a neighbour when he learnt that his grandchild was dead. This did not sound like a guilty man's behaviour. There was indeed evidence against Grooby, for his statement to the coroner accusing John Danks of the murder implicated himself, but it was possible that he had been afraid of being accused of murder and had lied to save himself. This might suggest guilt but might also mean that he was innocent but had feared that, in the circumstances, a court would not believe him. The judge said that while doing this would be 'very wicked conduct' it was possible, and said that the jury should remember that Grooby had made no attempt to flee the village, and had waited quietly to be arrested, which did not look like a guilty man's behaviour.

The judge said that if the baby had been murdered the culprit could just as easily have been the grandmother, Sarah Danks, or the young boy who lived in the house, as any of the three defendants. He concluded by saying that under English law the accused should always be given the benefit of any reasonable doubt.

Once the judge had made his speech the jury started their deliberations. As they considered their verdict the judge warned them that if any of the prisoners were convicted they would be hanged, and reminded them that it was better for twenty guilty people to go free than for one innocent person to be hanged.

After a short consultation the jury acquitted the prisoners. The judge congratulated them on a safe verdict which avoided the risk of hanging people who might be innocent.

The child was clearly murdered. It was the product of incest and two surgeons testified that it had been strangled but there was little evidence as to who had actually done the murder. Edward Grooby's confession, which he later retracted, did try to blame John Danks, but it was uncorroborated and so was worthless as evidence against John Danks. Edward Grooby's attempt to blame John Danks, while the other prisoners maintained their innocence, does suggest that it was Grooby who was guilty but does not prove it. As the judge pointed out Grooby might simply have panicked.

One possibility is that while only one person did the murder, the other four members of the household, except perhaps the young boy, well knew who did it, and so were accessories to murder. It would be impossible to keep a pregnancy secret in a village and so the Danks were deliberately open about it to avert suspicion when the murder was done.

Attempting to get the doctor in to deliver the baby and then arranging for a neighbour to deliver it would be part of this bluff.

Once Ann Barr and Hannah Proctor had left the house they would have waited for a period and then the baby would be strangled, probably by Grooby whose responsibility it was. Finally, to complete the bluff, John Danks would have fetched a neighbour. John Danks might well have been lying when he told the two women his account of events on the night the baby died.

Such a plot might seem a dangerous one as it depended on four people – or possibly five if the young boy was also implicated – keeping quiet, and Grooby did, on this reading of events nearly spoil things by panicking and trying to blame John Danks. But in the end the plot succeeded. In return for John Danks and his daughter and her half-brother spending a few months in prison awaiting trial, they disposed of a child whose very existence would have exposed them, and the boy himself if he had been allowed to live, to shame every day for the rest of their lives.

The Danks would never have recovered their social standing after this affair and the reputation of Fillongley itself must have suffered badly in this well-publicised scandal, but the absence of living proof would have been a major help to the Danks. Finally, of course, they had removed what would have been a considerable financial burden.

At the same assizes, a thirty-two-year-old servant, Elizabeth Elkington was also acquitted of murdering her newborn illegitimate child which had died of a fractured skull. However, evidence was presented that she suffered from fits and during one might have accidentally killed her child by dropping it on the floor. It is also possible that she deliberately murdered it but she was given the benefit of the doubt.

Courts in this period were usually sympathetic to people accused of infanticide, especially mothers, though there were exceptions to this rule. Two factors led to a high infanticide rate. Firstly, the absence of any reliable method of birth control or safe method of abortion meant that children born out of wedlock were normally an inevitable part of illicit sex. Secondly, most people lived very close to the survival line and an illegitimate child could be a heavy burden on a poor family, especially as social stigma could mean lost job opportunities.

In this period there were no women judges, lawyers or jurors but judges and jurymen had daughters and sisters and knew of the social and financial consequences that could arise from one mistake. Consequently, it was very rare for women accused of killing their babies to be convicted of murder except in the most extreme cases. Instead, some people were convicted of the lesser offence of concealing the birth of an illegitimate child, which carried a maximum penalty of two years in prison, but most such people were simply acquitted.

In the final analysis such a policy led to more infanticides as people learnt that in such cases the law was a 'paper tiger'. The authorities were perhaps happy for this to be so because it reduced the number of living testimonials to the contradictions between the code of ethics preached in churches and the realities of life.

CHAPTER 6

The Mysterious Case of the Mad Parson

Warwick, 1812

Warwick has been Warwickshire's county town since Saxon times, the county being named after it. In March 1812, one inhabitant was the Reverend William Brooks who was known as 'Mad Brooks' or the 'Mad Parson'. He appears to have been a sufferer from manic depression, alternating between spending up to thirteen weeks at a time in bed and wandering about wearing just a shirt, walking on tiptoe, looking 'wild', eating all kinds of food with his hands and impulsively threatening to shoot and kill people.

The Reverend Brooks lived in his own house. He let out part of it to a butcher, Thomas George, who had moved in in 1803 and who doubled as a minder during his landlord's manic episodes. In 1812, Thomas George employed a fourteen-year-old servant girl, Hannah Miller, who Brooks once threatened to shoot, calling her a 'saucy bitch'.

Another building in the same yard as the Reverend Brooks' house was used by a joiner William Tew as a workshop. Just after two in the afternoon on Thursday 5 March 1812, Tew heard a pistol shot. He went into the yard and found Hannah Miller sitting on the ground and supporting herself with her right hand.

William Tew asked Hannah Miller what was the matter, to be told: 'Parson Brooks has shot me with a pistol.' William Tew carried her into the kitchen of her master and his insane landlord. As he did so, he saw that blood was pouring through a hole in the back of her gown.

Later, the victim was taken to the 'front kitchen' and her assailant came to the door and stood with both hands behind him for about half a minute, wearing just a shirt. Eventually, two neighbours, Mrs Elizabeth Hammond and Mrs Ann Cooke, arrived and picked up the victim to help her upstairs to bed.

At the bottom of the stairs the two women helpers saw Brooks standing halfway up the stairs. Mrs Hammond said: 'You good for nothing villain! what have you done; get you to bed with you.'

The Reverend Brooks replied: 'Dare you come up?'

Perhaps foolishly, Mrs Hammond replied: 'I dare.' William Brooks put his left hand over his right and said: 'If you do I will shoot you.' He then drew his right hand back and Mrs Hammond saw something in it. She did not see what it was but was alarmed and turned to flee. She then heard a pistol shot which hit Hannah Miller under her left ear. Mrs Hammond and Mrs Cooke hastily fled the scene.

The victim staggered into the front kitchen and fell dead into William Tew's arms. Blood was pouring down her neck from the bullet wound under her ear. The police (or their 1812 equivalents) arrived and William Dore arrested the killer. He saw him standing at the top of the stairs and called to him to come down. He refused and Dore pursued him into Brooks' bedroom. There was a fight and Brooks punched Dore in the mouth but after a struggle, and with the help of others, Brooks was arrested.

John Squires, the Headborough ('police chief') of Warwick searched the prisoner's rooms. In a drawer he found two unloaded and recently fired pistols and noticed that the prisoner, who he had known as 'Mad Brooks' for twenty years, appeared drunk.

Meanwhile, the victim's body had been taken to the nearby

Warwick Shire Hall (built in 1753) where prisoners were tried. The author

Bear and Bacchus public house where surgeon William Blenkinsop did a post-mortem. Both wounds would have eventually been fatal.

On Friday 6 March 1812 a coroner's inquest returned a verdict that the victim had been murdered by the Reverend William Brooks. He was brought to trial at the Warwick Lent Assizes on Thursday 2 April 1812, the judge being Sir John Bayley.

The prosecution counsel, Mr Clarke, briefly outlined what had happened and seven witnesses – William Tew, Mrs Hammond, Mrs Cooke, William Dore, John Squires, Thomas George and Surgeon Blenkinsop – gave their evidence. Apart from describing the killing, the main focus was naturally on whether the prisoner was insane. William Tew, Mrs Hammond, Mrs Cooke, William Dore, John Squires and Thomas George all testified to him being 'mad', though Thomas George said that the prisoner was relatively sane as regards money matters.

The judge summed up, ruling that the prisoner should be acquitted as he was 'insane'. The jury agreed and the Reverend William Brooks was ordered to be detained at His Majesty's Pleasure.

The facts of this case as outlined in the *Warwick Advertiser*, from which other newspapers took their shorter reports, appear simple but they leave behind a mystery. Just who was the Reverend William Brooks? Was he an Anglican or a non-conformist clergyman? Had he ever held a parish or even a

On Saturday last, a Coroner's inquest was held on the body of Hannah Miller, who on the Thursday preceding was shot by the Rev. W. Brookes, of this Borough, which after a long and patient investigation, returned a verdict of *Wilful Murder*.—From motives of peculiar delicacy, we have forborne to enter, prematurely, into the detail of this melancholy transaction.—The great and awful question will shortly be determined before a competent tribunal—when the trial, at length, will be communicated to our readers.

Report of the Hannah Miller inquest, *Warwick Advertiser*, 14 March 1812.
Birmingham Library

curacy? Who were his parents and where did he come from? When was he born – the trial records fail to disclose his age – and when did he eventually die?

Clerical dictionaries such as Crockford's and its predecessors do not go back far enough to be of help. The *alumni* records of Oxford and Cambridge disclose a number of graduates of the right name and period including at least one who never held any living but they are inconclusive. The *Warwick Advertiser* was rather coy in its accounts of the case so what family scandal lay behind it?

Warwick remains a charming town and still houses many buildings that were there in 1812.

CHAPTER 7

The Man who was Tried Twice

Castle Bromwich & Sutton Coldfield, 1817

I n 1817 the *Tyburn House* was a well known Castle Bromwich pub standing in open country. On the evening and night of 26/27 May 1817 a local Friendly Society held its annual dance there. One attendee was twenty-year-old Mary Ashford. Her father was a gardener and lived in Erdington, as did her grandfather, but Mary lived with her uncle at Langley in the parish of Sutton Coldfield. At the dance Mary wore fresh clothes consisting of a clean cotton frock, a white muslin spencer (a type of close-fitting jacket or bodice), a pair of cotton stockings and a new pair of shoes.

The Tyburn House, Castle Bromwich, today. The author

Tyburn at the time of the murder. Birmingham Library

To avoid soiling her party clothes Mary had left them, in a
bundle, with a friend, Hannah Cox, who was a servant for a Mr
Machell of Erdington and who lodged with Hannah's mother-in-
law, Mrs Butler. Mary had left her best clothes with her friend at
ten in the morning on the day of the dance. Having gone to
Birmingham market, at six in the evening she called on her friend
at Mr Machell's house. The two girls went to Mrs Butler's and
Mary changed into her fresh clothes leaving her everyday clothes,
which were a pink frock or gown, a red muslin spencer, another
pair of stockings and old shoes there.

The two girls left for the dance at eight in the evening.

Mary Ashford. Birmingham Library

Another attendee was Abraham Thornton, a twenty-five-year-old Castle Bromwich bricklayer whose father was a local farmer. Abraham was attracted to Mary and they spent much time dancing but, according to what a local farmer's son, Joseph Cooke, later said, Thornton had more on his mind, telling Cooke: 'I have been connected with her sister three times, and I will with her, or I'll die by it.' Despite knowing Mary Ashford well, Cooke failed to warn her of this boast.

At between eleven and twelve at night Mary Ashford and Abraham Thornton left the dance. Initially, they were in company with Hannah Cox and Benjamin Carter, a local farmer's son. Benjamin Carter soon left them to briefly return to the dance and Hannah left them at a spot 'between Mr Reeve's and the 'Old Cuckoo'; and then returned to her lodgings.

Having left the dance, Benjamin Carter overtook Mary Ashford and Abraham Thornton and walked with them for a while before their ways parted. At about three in the morning on 27 May John Hompidge, a Witton man, who was courting the daughter of a Mr Reynolds who lived near Penn's Mills, saw and heard Thornton in conversation with a young woman, presumably Mary Ashford. They were sitting on a stile leading to Bell Lane. John Hompidge knew Thornton and they exchanged greetings but the woman hid her head.

At about half three Thomas Aspree, an Erdington man, saw Mary Ashford on her own walking very fast towards Erdington. Later Mary knocked on Mrs Butler's door and was let in. Mary changed into her old clothes though she kept her new shoes on. The clock in the house said that it was twenty to five but John Webster (see below) later checked it against his watch which was

Abraham Thornton. Birmingham Library

very accurate and which kept 'Birmingham time' – before the coming of the railways there was no national system of time-keeping. He found that Mrs Butler's clock was forty minutes fast, thus making the time Mary arrived there four o'clock. Mary told Hannah that she had gone to her grandfather's but in fact she had been at her uncle's, though for much of the time she had actually been with Abraham Thornton.

After staying for a quarter of an hour Mary Ashford left her friend again at a quarter past four. John Chesterton, a waggoner for Mr Greensall, a local farmer, had got up at two o'clock, 'fettled' (girded up) his master's horses, and then took them to a pit in Bell Lane to water them. At about ten past four he saw Mary Ashford, who he knew well. At about this time Joseph Dawson, a local labourer, saw Mary and at about twenty past four Thomas Broadhurst saw her walking towards Penn's Mills.

At about half past four, according to the local clocks, William Jennings, a Birmingham milkman, and his wife Martha, who had been buying milk, saw Thornton between Erdington and Castle Bromwich. Other people also saw him in this area at about the same time or later or corroborated the evidence of those who had including Jane Heaton; John Haydon, a gamekeeper who saw Thornton near Zachariah Twamley's stables and mill just outside Castle Bromwich; John Holden and his son, John Holden Junior, with whose clock the Jennings had checked the time; John Woodcock; and James White who saw Thornton in Castle Bromwich at about twenty past five. William Twamley and William Crampton later checked the local clocks finding that they were about a quarter of an hour ahead of Birmingham time.

On the morning of 27 May 1817 a labourer, George Jackson, had left his Hurst Street, Birmingham, home to walk to his Sutton

Pool where Mary Ashford's body was discovered. Birmingham Library

Coldfield workplace. As he reached Moor Street he heard the clock on St Martin's, parish church, strike five. On his way to work he passed Erdington Workhouse and then turned off Bell Lane onto a footpath. As he passed a water-filled pit, which was in a field of clover by the lane, he noticed a bonnet, a pair of shoes and a bundle lying close by the edge of the slope which led down to the pit. He investigated, to find that one of the shoes was covered in blood. He was frightened and ran to the nearest house for help.

The householder, William Lavell, went with Jackson to the pit and stayed there to take care of the items Jackson had found while Jackson went to Penn's Mills, a nearby wire factory, for more help. George Jackson told the people at Penn's Mills about what he had found and then went onto his own workplace.

Meanwhile, a number of workers at Penn's Mills, including

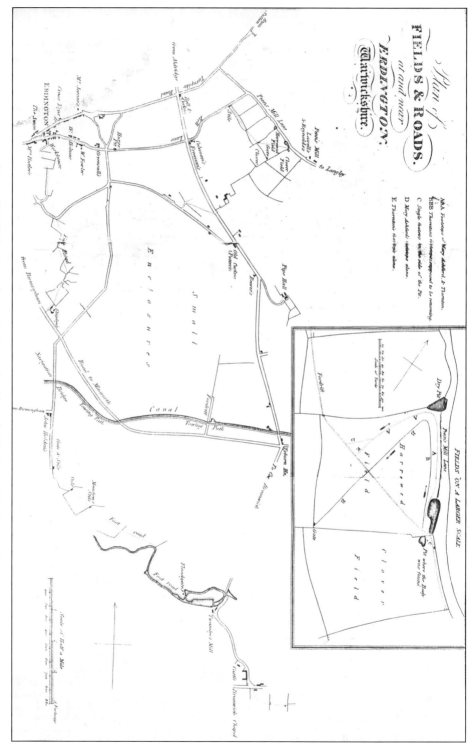

Map of 1819 showing places relating to the Mary Ashford case. Birmingham Library

Joseph Bird and James Simmonds, went to join Lavell. Simmonds took a heel rake and a pair of long reins and used them to drag the pit. At eight in the morning on 27 May, he managed to drag up a body that had been lying in the pit. It was that of Mary Ashford and was wearing a red spencer, a pink gown and a pair of stockings.

Various footmarks were found in the nearby fields, indicating that Mary Ashford's attacker had chased her across the fields before catching her. The gap between the footmarks clearly showed that both she and her assailant had been running. There was a single deep footmark by the pool's edge, suggesting that her attacker had deliberately thrown her in. A single set of men's footprints led away from the pit towards Castle Bromwich. William Lavell and Joseph Bird examined the footprints discovering that the man's were those of a pair of shoes, one of which had two nails in it, while the woman's footmarks matched those made by the shoes Jackson had found by the side of the pit. To avoid rain damaging the footprints Lavell and Bird protected them with boards and a local magistrate, William Bedford, posted guards to fend off sightseers.

John Webster, the owner of Penn's Mills, found a particularly important piece of evidence, the impression of a human figure in the grass at a spot some forty yards from the pit. The legs were extended and the arms were stretched out at full length. Between the leg marks were the marks of knees and of a man's shoes. There was also a large bloodstain. This was later interpreted as evidence that Mary Ashford had been raped and that she had been a virgin.

The victim's body was taken to William Lavell's house. John Webster saw it there and noticed marks on each arm which seemed to have been made by the grasp of a man's hand. William Lavell's wife, Frances, and a local woman, Mary Smith, undressed the body and examined it. The lower parts were very bloodstained as was the seat of the gown, which had to be torn from the victim's body.

George Freer, a Birmingham surgeon, and Mr Hortin, a Sutton Coldfield surgeon, were called to examine the body further and they arrived at the Lavells' house on the evening of 27 May. They briefly looked at the body but it was already too dark to examine it properly. Gaslight had been invented in 1817 but it was not in general use and no surgeon could properly examine a body under candlelight.

The next morning Freer opened the victim's body. He found about half a pint of water and some chickweed in the stomach and as a result of his examination concluded that she had died from drowning. There were no marks of violence upon the body other than those immediately associated with the rape.

Suspicion had quickly fallen on Abraham Thornton and on the morning of the 27th, the day the body was found, Daniel Clarke, the publican of the *Tyburn House*, had gone to Castle Bromwich where he had met Thornton who he advised to come peacefully to the Tyburn House and give himself up to the authorities. The suspect admitted to having been with the victim until nearly four in the morning but denied murder.

Thomas Dale, an Assistant Constable of Birmingham, and William Benson, arrested Thornton. They took one of his shoes, which had two nails in it, and found it matched the appropriate footprints. They and William Bedford, the magistrate who had charged Thornton with murder, also later alleged that Thornton had admitted to having had sex with the victim though he denied murder.

Abraham Thornton was charged with murder and rape and a coroner's inquest returned a verdict that the victim had been murdered by the prisoner, who was brought to trial at the Warwick Summer Assizes on Friday 8 August 1817. The judge was Sir George Sowley and the twelve-man jury consisted of eight farmers, a draper, a steelworker, a comb maker and a needle worker.

The prosecution counsel were Mr Clarke, Mr Copley and Mr Perkins. Messrs Reader and Reynolds defended the prisoner. Mr Clarke opened the prosecution case with a speech in which he stressed that the prisoner had been with the victim on the night of the murder; that his shoe matched the footprints found in the field; that he had earlier boasted of his intentions to have sex with the victim; and that he had later confessed to having done so though he had denied murder.

Twenty witnesses: Hannah Cox, Benjamin Carter, John Hompidge, Thomas Aspree, John Chesterton, Joseph Dawson, Thomas Broadhurst, George Jackson, William Lavell, Joseph Bird, James Simmonds, John Webster, Frances Lavell, Mary Smith, William Bedford, Thomas Dale, William Benson, Joseph Cooke, Daniel Clarke, and Surgeon Freer – testified for the prosecution.

After the prosecution had finished the defence produced eleven witnesses. Ten attested that the accused had been in Castle Bromwich at a time shortly after the victim was last seen alive and therefore had a good alibi, these being William and Martha Jennings, Jane Heaton, John Holden senior and junior, William Twamley, John Haydon, John Woodcock, William Crampton and

James White. Saddest of all, Mary Ashford's maternal grand-father, William Coleman, admitted to the court that his granddaughter had lied to her friend Hannah Cox about her whereabouts before she came to her house and changed on the morning of the murder, presumably out of shame at spending so long in Thornton's company.

The judge then summed up. While making it clear that the victim had been murdered, he pointed out the strength of the prisoner's alibi. The all-male jury took just a few minutes to acquit Thornton of both murder and rape.

This controversial acquittal produced intense public outrage. A few people protested that Thornton had had a good alibi but they were shouted down by people such as the Reverend Luke Booker of Dudley, who essentially accused Thornton's defenders of approving of the murder.

Although this situation is currently in the process of being changed for many years it has been an English legal principle that once someone has been acquitted they cannot be tried again on the same charge. However, in 1817 there still existed a procedure called the 'Appeal of Murder'. If a person accused of murder was acquitted, the victim's nearest relative could appeal to the Court of King's Bench which could order a retrial. Victims of larceny, arson or rape could also appeal to this court if the person accused of the crime against them had been acquitted.

The last successful use of an Appeal of Murder had been the case of Christopher Slaughterford. He had been accused of killing his fiancee Jane Young in October 1708 and had been acquitted at the 1709 Surrey Lent Assizes. The victim's family had made an Appeal of Murder against him and he had been tried before Lord Chief Justice Holt and a fresh jury at the Court of King's Bench in London which convicted him of murder. He was hanged on 1 July 1709 and died protesting his innocence.

The Appeal of Murder had become obsolete in the eighteenth century. Although the courts could still be biased and make mistakes, the 'robber barons' and large-scale criminal gangs, against whose physical intimidation of local courts the procedure had been designed to guard, had passed into history by 1817. However, it was still legal and a public collection raised the money with which Mary Ashford's seventeen-year-old Staffordshire labourer brother William Ashford could make an Appeal of Murder against Thornton.

On 10 October 1817 the Sheriff of Warwickshire received a Writ of Appeal and Thornton was rearrested and returned to Warwick Gaol. In November 1817 a writ of *habeas corpus* was issued and on 17 November 1817 the prisoner appeared before the Lord Chief Justice, Lord Ellenborough, and four other senior judges at the Court of King's Bench. William Ashford's counsel were Mr Clarke, who been a prosecution counsel at the first trial, and Messrs Gurney, Richardson and Chitty. The prisoner's lawyers were, again, Messrs Reader and Reynolds.

Mr Le Blanc, the Clerk to the Crown Office, read out the charge against the prisoner who replied: 'Not Guilty and I am ready to defend the same with my body.' In other words he was claiming the right to 'Trial by Combat'.

The right to Trial by Combat had been introduced into England by the Normans. One circumstance in which it could be claimed was in defence against an Appeal of Murder. In medieval times it had allegedly been believed that a person with right on their side would fight better than someone with a guilty conscience. More cynical observers have suggested that it was introduced to protect combat-trained Norman knights from justice seeking Saxons. Trial by Combat was even more obsolete than the Appeal of Murder. The last time anyone had claimed the right to it had been in 1632, before the Civil War, during the brief period of Charles I's personal rule when there had been self conscious efforts to revive the feudal system. Even then various excuses had been made and the fight had been cancelled.

If the 1817 fight had gone ahead William Ashford and the prisoner would have had to fight, starting at sunrise. If Ashford killed Thornton this would mean that Thornton was guilty. If Thornton gave in before nightfall the prisoner would have been found guilty and hanged. If the prisoner killed Ashford, forced him to give in, or kept on fighting until nightfall, he would be found innocent.

William Ashford's counsel, Mr Clarke, asked how could Thornton prove he was innocent of killing the sister by killing her brother? Lord Ellenborough, who was a famous reactionary, pointed out that killing someone in a judicial duel was not murder.

There were prolonged and tedious legal deliberations centring on ways of denying the prisoner's right to Trial by Combat. Medieval law books were consulted dating back to the twelfth century when the feudal system was still in full force and England was a country of arrogant Norman barons and resentful Saxon serfs, rather than the England of 1817 in which, despite ferocious class divisions, both rulers and ruled were Englishmen.

(Opposite) The title page of a contemporary pamphlet about the Mary Ashford case. Birmingham Library

OBSERVATIONS

UPON THE CASE OF

ABRAHAM THORNTON,

WHO WAS

TRIED AT WARWICK, AUGUST 8, 1817,

FOR **THE** MURDER OF

MARY ASHFORD:

SHEWING THE

DANGER OF PRESSING PRESUMPTIVE EVIDENCE TOO FAR,

TOGETHER WITH

THE ONLY TRUE AND AUTHENTIC ACCOUNT YET PUBLISHED
OF THE EVIDENCE GIVEN AT THE TRIAL, THE
EXAMINATION OF THE PRISONER, &c.

AND

A CORRECT PLAN OF THE LOCUS IN QUO.

SECOND EDITION.

BY EDWARD HOLROYD,

OF GRAY'S INN.

" Judging is, as it were, balancing an account, and determining on which
" side the odds lie. If, therefore, either be huddled up in haste, and several
" of the sums, that should have gone into the account be overlooked, and left
" out, this precipitancy causes as wrong a judgment, as if it were a perfect igno-
" rance. To check this precipitancy, our understanding and reason were given
" us, if we will make a right use of it, to search, and see, and then judge
" thereupon."—LOCKE.

LONDON:

PRINTED FOR J. MAWMAN, 39, LUDGATE STREET.

1819.

In the Middle Ages it had been a legal rule that no one could claim the right to Trial by Combat in defence to an Appeal of Murder if they had been caught red-handed, for instance, if they had been found at the scene of the murder with a bloodstained knife in their hands. They might still protest their innocence but they would have to face a fresh jury. However, as his counsel pointed out, Thornton had produced a strong alibi. Also, in the Middle Ages one could not claim Trial by Combat against certain people including women, anyone over sixty, priests, peers of the realm and citizens of London. Even in the days when Trials by Combat actually happened, the City of London had been powerful enough to gain such an exemption. However, no such exemption was found to cover this case.

On 16 April 1818, the Court of King's Bench finally decided that if William Ashford had the right to make an Appeal of Murder, Abraham Thornton had the right to claim Trial by Combat. On 20 April 1818, William Ashford dropped his appeal and the prisoner was freed and returned home.

The strain of the two trials and the legal fees had first impoverished and then killed Abraham Thornton's farmer father. Thornton was ostracised by the local community and emigrated to the USA.

A widespread report appeared that before he sailed a Liverpool prostitute picked Thornton's pockets and found a letter which he had intended to post from America. In it he supposedly confessed to having raped his victim and then killed her because he feared a rape charge, rape also being a capital offence. The letter turned out to be a forgery.

In 1819, the authorities abolished both the Appeal of Murder and Trial by Combat. Mary Ashford was buried in Sutton Coldfield's medieval churchyard and her alleged killer vanished from history.

Was Abraham Thornton guilty or was the killer another man who just happened to be wearing shoes which resembled his? The mystery has produced intense speculation. It can only be said that modern clocks are more accurate, DNA testing exists today and forensic evidence such as that of the footprints would be backed up by evidence as to what proportion of men possessed such shoes.

The *Tyburn House* public house still exists and today stands in a completely urbanised area. The present building dates from the 1930s.

Chapter 8

A Robbery

Birmingham, 1825

On Saturday 10 December 1825, the *Birmingham Journal* reported that 'We have to detail the particulars of a crime committed in this town on Tuesday last more horrible than any it has yet devolved upon us to record in this vicinity.' *The Birmingham Journal* had only been established earlier that year, being Birmingham's second successful newspaper.

On Tuesday 6 December 1825, at between ten and eleven in the evening, an Irish labourer, Michael Ford, aged twenty-six, from County Clare, had entered Richard Perry's 'huckster's shop' (general stores) in Birmingham's Mary Ann Street. Michael Ford, who already owed Perry money, bought a few small items and then asked to buy some pork. Perry cut him some pork with a cleaver and then put the cleaver down.

While Perry had his back turned Ford put his hands into the cash drawer under the counter. Perry noticed and moved to stop him. Michael Ford seized the cleaver and attacked Perry with it, striking him several blows on the head. The victim fell to the floor.

Michael Ford then allegedly picked Perry's pockets and started to empty the cash drawer but he accidentally dropped it on the floor. The noise was heard by Perry's nineteen-year-old niece, Mary Perry who had been in the back kitchen. She rushed into the shop and seeing what had happened cried out: 'You Villain! You've murdered my uncle!' Michael Ford tried to attack her with the cleaver but Mary wrenched it from him and threw him to the ground. She then ran into the street and shouted for help. Meanwhile, Ford got up, followed her out into the street and made his escape.

Richard Perry's wife, Hannah arrived, having been in the cellar. The two women sent for a surgeon, Francis Russell Elkington, but the victim's wounds proved fatal and he died on Thursday 8 December 1825.

The Birmingham police sent handbills out across the country

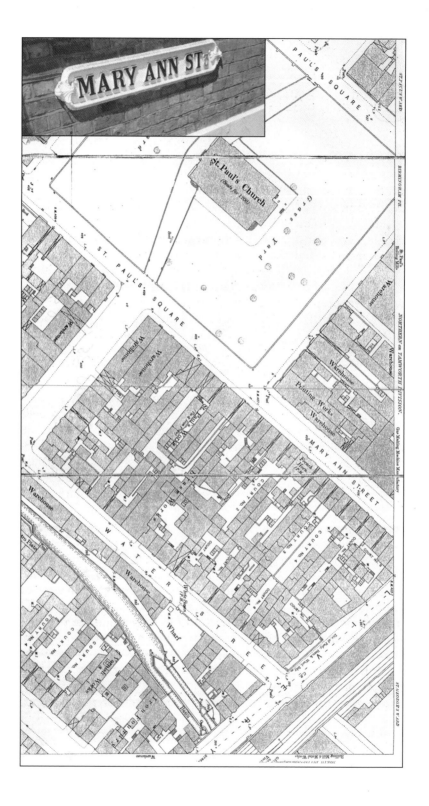

describing Ford's appearance and offering a £50 reward (c.£10,000 today) for his arrest. The suspect was about five foot, seven inches tall. He had a 'fair complexion, long visage and light hair'. His notable features included a 'hole in the right cheek out of which arises a lump which frequently wants opening, and he sometimes had a patch upon it; he has lost two of the teeth on the right side of his mouth'. This deformity had been caused by an overloaded gun backfiring. The fourth finger of Ford's hand had been amputated at the second joint and the little finger of the same hand was permanently bent. At the time of the attack he was wearing a blue coat, light corded breeches, blue stockings and very old shoes.

The Birmingham police realised that Ford would probably try to flee to Ireland and among those to whom they sent handbills were the Liverpool police. On Saturday 10 December, Mr Harold Adkins, the keeper of Birmingham Prison, received information from Mr Miller, the Liverpool police chief that the suspect had been caught in Liverpool. A Liverpool police officer, Thomas Boughey, had seen Ford on the pier head of St George's Dock and recognised him from the handbills. As Ford tried to board the Dublin steam packet (steamship), Boughey arrested him.

Michael Ford claimed to be John Hembury and denied ever having been to Birmingham in his life but Miller showed him the handbills, with his description written on them, and he fell silent. On Monday 12 December 1825, Ford was taken back to Birmingham on the night mailcoach by Adkins who had been sent to fetch him. Mr Boughey accompanied them. Only some five shillings in silver and a few half pence were found on Ford. The rest of the stolen money had presumably gone to pay for going from Birmingham to Liverpool and for his passage to Ireland.

The coroner's inquest on the victim was opened at ten on Monday morning in the *Woolpack Inn* in Birmingham's Moor Street, before the coroner, Mr J W Whateley. Mr Whateley and his jury first went to the Perrys' house and shop to inspect the dead body. They then returned to the *Woolpack* and the prisoner was brought before them, heavily chained and very dejected. During the inquest he maintained a 'stoical indifference', even when the bloodstained murder weapon was produced.

Evidence was given by the victim's niece and widow, by some people who helped to carry the body from the shop into the back

Opposite: Map dated 1889 showing the Mary Ann Street area of Birmingham. Ordnance Survey/The author

kitchen, by surgeon Elkington and by the Liverpool police officer
Boughey. After hearing this evidence the jury returned a verdict
that Richard Perry had been murdered by Michael Ford.

The coroner told the journalists at the inquest that they would
be banned from taking notes of the evidence to avoid prejudicing
the subsequent trial and that if they did so they would be
prosecuted. Both the *Birmingham Journal* and the *Birmingham
Gazette* complied with the letter of this order and did not print
any details of the evidence given by the various witnesses, but
they evaded its spirit by printing full accounts of the murder
based on information they had gathered outside the courtroom.
The newspapers argued that although even the most accurate
account of inquest proceedings could prejudice a subsequent
trial jury against a prisoner, it was necessary for them to accu-
rately report them to avoid the spread of rumours which could
do far more damage. They also argued that such a ban infringed
press freedom which was the best security for the 'life and liberty
of the subject'. The American and French revolutions were
within living memory and only a small minority of the population
could vote.

The newspapers said that they would take legal action to deter-
mine the legality of the coroner's order. No information is
available as to the result of this action but it seems to have been
successful since in later murder cases the Birmingham local
papers gave full accounts of inquest proceedings.

Michael Ford was tried at the Warwick Lent Assizes on Friday
25 March 1826. The judge was Mr Justice Littledale and the trial
opened just before nine in the morning. The prisoner wore a blue
coat, a buff waistcoat and a darkish coloured silk cravat. The press
were unable to see his feet.

The first prosecution witness was the victim's niece, Mary
Perry, who was dressed in deep mourning black and appeared
very distressed. She was described in court as being a 'frail and
delicate looking' young woman. She explained that she lived with
her uncle at his Mary Ann Street shop, and had seen the prisoner
there many times. She had heard him arrive at about twenty past
ten on Tuesday 6 December 1825 and had gone into the shop to
see who was there. She saw Ford, the victim and his wife there and
heard the accused ask the victim for some pork. The witness then
returned to the kitchen and the victim's wife went to the cellar. A
minute or two later, Mary heard a noise which sounded like
someone chopping pork and was probably the noise of the attack.
Then she heard the money drawer falling on the floor and coins
clattering.

Mary Perry left the kitchen and went through the sitting room to the shop. The door between the sitting room and the shop was open and as she approached it Ford came towards her with the cleaver. She screamed: 'You villain! You've murdered my uncle!' The prisoner then attacked her but she wrenched the cleaver from his hands, threw it on the floor and then threw Ford to the floor. Mary then ran into the street screaming: 'Murder!' The alleged killer ran out too and escaped. When the witness came back into the shop she saw her uncle lying behind the counter with blood pouring from his head. The victim's wife, Mary's aunt, was in with her husband.

The cleaver was shown to the court. It was a foot long with a rounded end. The black straw hat which the victim had been wearing when he was murdered was also produced in court. It had two cuts in it. The witness identified both the cleaver and the hat, which she had made herself, as her uncle's. Finally, she confirmed that the prisoner was indeed Michael Ford.

The next witness was the victim's widow Hannah, who was also very distressed. She said that she had known the prisoner for three weeks before the murder. The victim had employed him to carry potatoes but he had only actually come into the house as opposed to the shop once, on the morning before the murder.

Michael Ford had entered the shop at about half ten in the evening, as Mr Perry was fastening up the shutters and closing up. He first asked for a loaf, half an ounce of coffee, half a pound of bacon, a quarter of sugar and some potatoes. These were placed on the counter. The prisoner also asked for some pork and the victim chopped it for him and then put the cleaver on a bench on the customer's side of the counter. The victim then went to his side of the counter and his wife went to the cellar. The Perrys and Ford had been talking and joking for 'some time'.

While Hannah Perry was in the cellar she heard the money drawer fall on the floor. She ran up to the shop and got there in time to see Ford fleeing from the shop. Her niece then came in and told her about the attack.

Hannah and Mary Perry found Richard Perry lying behind the counter with blood pouring from him. He never recovered consciousness. The articles Ford had asked for were still on the counter except for the potatoes which had fallen on the floor. The widow concluded that she recognised the prisoner and that her shop was widely used by Birmingham's Irish community.

The third witness, Ann Smith, testified that she had heard Mary Perry yell out that a murder had happened. She went into the shop and saw the scene as described by Mary and Hannah

Perry. John Walthew then told the court that he too had heard Mary Perry's shouts and had gone for help.

William Webb, who had been at a nearby pub, *The Jolly Sailor*, stated that he had seen Ford there on the night of the murder and that Ford had left the pub at ten in the evening.

Mary Groutage then testified that she had seen a man lurking about the Perrys' premises at between ten and eleven on the evening of the murder. The man had then gone into the shop and the victim had served him with some articles.

The seventh witness was the Surgeon, Elkington. He had got to the Perrys' house at a quarter to eleven on the murder night. Richard Perry had been placed on a back kitchen chair and was covered in blood. Elkington had him taken up stairs and examined his head. There was a six-inch-long and inch-deep wound on the front of the head which had gone through the skull and into the brain. Another wound on the back of the head had also penetrated the brain. Either wound alone would have been fatal and both could have been made by the cleaver produced in court.

Mr Adkins, the keeper of Birmingham Prison, then told the court how he had arrested the prisoner in Liverpool. The ninth and last witness, Thomas Boughey, the Liverpool police officer who had spotted the prisoner boarding the Dublin steam packet, then gave his evidence.

The prosecution then closed its case. Michael Ford had no lawyer. He gave a written testimonial to a court official who read it out for him. It said that he had been working in Birmingham and admitted to having shopped at the Perrys' shop on the night of the murder. After buying the articles he wanted he left them in the shop by arrangement, intending to collect them in the morning. He then left but returned again after hearing shouts to learn about the murder. He panicked, fearing that he might be made a scapegoat and tried to flee to Ireland. He admitted that doing this was wrong but pointed out that he was a friendless man in a strange city. Michael Ford then pleaded for mercy, saying that he would never have killed the victim, who had been very kind to him. The prisoner called one witness, Mr Tatnall, the Governor of Warwick Gaol, in his defence. Mr Tatnall testified that while Ford was in custody he had seemed to be a good tempered, quiet and inoffensive man.

The judge then summed up. The jury took just five minutes to convict the prisoner of murder and the judge then sentenced him to death. The prisoner burst into tears.

On the second Saturday after the trial, 2 April 1826, Ford yielded to the persuasions or moral pressure of the High Sheriff of

Mary Ann Street where Michael Ford allegedly murdered Richard Perry.
The author

Warwickshire and confessed to the murder. In a letter he sent to the Reverend Ambrose Boise of Ennis in County Clare, he said that he had originally just intended robbery and had done the murder in panic. In a letter to his wife, Mary, he asked her to remarry as soon as possible and hoped that her next husband would be a better man than himself. He asked her to take good care of their infant child.

Although Ford was a Roman Catholic he attended divine service in the Anglican prison chapel with the other prisoners though he spent his time, reading a Catholic Missal. At ten on Sunday 3 April, the night before the hanging, he went to bed, waking up at midnight screaming about the jury's conduct. At four in the morning of Monday 4 April, Ford was visited by a Catholic priest, the Reverend Turville, to whom he gave the letters addressed to the Reverend Boise and to his wife asking that he first give them to the High Sheriff. The prisoner ate a hearty breakfast at half past seven that morning. At a quarter to ten he was taken to the 'press room' of Warwick Gaol to have his arms pinioned in front of him. Mr Tatnall, the prison governor, gave the condemned man two glasses of wine and Ford thanked him for his humanity.

At ten that morning 'the melancholy procession, headed by the officers of justice moved towards the place of execution'. The prisoner was attended on the scaffold by the Anglican Reverend Laugharne and the Catholic Reverend Turville, with the latter of whom he prayed until the executioner put the rope around his neck and generally prepared the gallows. The Reverend Turville stepped down from the gallows and Ford was given a handkerchief and told to drop it when he was ready to be hanged. He dropped it before the hangman was ready to withdraw the bolt. Mr Tatnall then stepped up and gave him the handkerchief back. The prisoner then spent some minutes praying aloud, at first in English but then in his native Irish Gaelic. Michael Ford then dropped the handkerchief again, the hangman withdrew the bolt and the accused was hanged. He died after a minute of convulsions and his body was sent for dissection at Birmingham General Hospital.

The seventeenth century *Fox & Grapes*, one of the few buildings left in central Birmingham that Michael Ford would have recognised. The author

The statue of Nelson, erected in 1809 and still standing in the Bullring.
The author

This case may seem open and shut but there was, at least by modern standards, one glaring weakness which a good defence lawyer would have exposed. The chief witnesses were the victim's widow and niece and there was no direct corroboration of their account of the actual murder. If such evidence was given today, any competent defence lawyer would suggest that Mary and Hannah Perry were the culprits and had framed a friendless Irish labourer of odd appearance. As for the prisoner's panic-stricken flight, this might have represented fear rather than guilt, as the prisoner himself had claimed. Hannah and Mary Perry's conspicuous grief might well have merely been a mask. Such things have happened. In fact, Michael Ford was probably guilty though it should be said that in this period, public attitudes towards the Catholic Irish were remarkably similar to modern attitudes towards black people. Nowadays forensic science is far more advanced enabling courts to demand stronger evidence without jeopardising the public safety. In the final analysis we cannot judge the early nineteenth century by twenty-first century standards.

The Jolly Sailor disappeared not long after 1826, for it is not listed in 1840s Birmingham trade directories. *The Woolpack* where the inquest was held was a well-known hotel and survived until it fell victim to 1950s redevelopment. Mary Ann Street still exists running between Livery Street and St Paul's Square in Hockley, which houses St Paul's Church and most of central Birmingham's few other remaining eighteenth century buildings.

CHAPTER 9

Revenge

Birmingham, 1838

In 1836, Birmingham was a rapidly expanding, brash industrial city. One Birmingham entrepreneur was twenty-six-year-old master plated spoon maker William Devey whose workshop was in Little Hampton Street in Hockley and who was married with one child.

Meanwhile, on 8 November 1836 George Askey, a former master die sinker, got work with Charles Rowley, a master stamper and piercer. Askey was contracted to work for Rowley from seven in the morning to seven in the evening in summer with an hour for breakfast and an hour for dinner; and from eight to seven in the winter with an hour for dinner.

Hearing that Askey had got a job with Rowley, Devey asked Askey to work for him as well – on the side. Askey agreed and would work for Devey in the morning and evenings, sometimes in his own time but at other times when he should have been working for Rowley, to whom he was contracted. At such times he would claim to be sick. Askey even acted as an industrial spy and 'introduced the improvements of Mr Rowley into the dies of the defendant'.

Charles Rowley found out what was happening. In May 1837, a magistrate gaoled Askey for a month for neglecting his work. Rowley then sued Devey for 'seducing the hired servant of the plaintiff to leave his master's work'. Devey tried to persuade Askey to perjure himself in court but a chastened Askey refused and the case was heard in the nisi prius court at Warwick Lent Assizes on Saturday 24 March 1838. The judge was Sir J A Park, the prosecution counsel were Mr Sergeant Goulbourn and Mr Waddington, and the defence counsel were Mr Sergeant Adams and Mr E L Williams.

The main witness was Askey. There were other witnesses, some of whom were not called, including Joseph Davenport, the landlord of the *Pheasant* pub in Little Hampton Street. Eventually Devey was ordered to pay Rowley £2 in compensation (c.£500 today).

Parallel to this case a totally different William Devey, a Surrey coal merchant, went bankrupt and his name appeared in the *London Gazette*. Word of this came to Birmingham and George Redfern, a senior Birmingham police official, got confused over the names and warned the Birmingham Gas Light Company who sent the bailiffs in to collect the money the Birmingham William Devey owed them, despite only being owed one quarter's rent.

The Birmingham Devey blamed Davenport for his largely self-inflicted wrongs. On the evening of Tuesday 3 April 1838 he visited a Birmingham factor or merchant, George Leeson of St George's Terrace, from whom he rented machinery, at Leeson's Little Hampton Street warehouse. He told Leeson: 'Davenport was the greatest enemy he had, and he (Devey) had been the best friend Davenport ever had.' George Leeson told Devey that from what he knew of Davenport this was probably untrue but Devey then blamed Davenport for sending the Gas Company after him. On the morning of Wednesday 4 April 1838 Devey told an employee, Frederick Watson, that he had been 'gazetted' as a bankrupt and might have to 'go out of the way for a time.'

At three in the afternoon, on Wednesday 4 April 1838, Devey visited a Weaman Street gun and pistol makers that was kept by Emma Davis and her sister Caroline Webley. William Devey asked to buy a pair of pistols and they sold him a pair of single shot pistols for ten shillings and sixpence (c.£100 today). He also asked to buy bullets and they told him to return in half an hour when they would have cast them. He returned after an hour and they sold him twenty-eight bullets which weighed about half a pound. They also gave him some copper caps and showed him how to load the gun. They asked no questions as to its purpose.

At about six in the evening that Wednesday Devey visited *The Salutation* on Snow Hill with a friend, Benjamin Clulee. Devey bought a glass of gin and water for Clulee but refused any drinks for himself. They talked, Devey blaming Joseph Davenport for bringing his creditors down upon him despite Devey having been friendly to him; and spoke of revenge. Benjamin Clulee told him that Davenport was not a bad man and that Devey had brought his troubles upon himself and should have 'done with courts of law and attend to his business'.

Later that same evening Frederick Watson saw Devey following Davenport along the 'horse road' (Little Hampton Street). At about seven Davenport entered William Batkin's locksmith's shop asking for Mr Batkin. One of Batkin's workers, Samuel Farrington, whose home address was No. 2, Union Court, Lower Tower Street, went to fetch Batkin from the workshop leaving Davenport on his own in the shop. About a minute later

Farrington returned to the shop and saw Devey walk in with a pistol in each hand. Devey walked up to Davenport and said: 'Damn your eyes. You have been the ruin of me.' Joseph Davenport replied: 'What do you follow me for?' Devey threatened, saying: 'Now I will settle you', to be asked: 'What have I done to you?' Devey then raised his right hand and fired his pistol at his former friend and imagined persecutor. The gun initially failed to go off and Davenport tried to flee into Batkin's sitting room but before he could even grasp the door Devey fired again with the same gun, and this time it went off, hitting Davenport in the head, penetrating his brain and killing him instantly.

George Leeson had seen Devey enter Batkin's shop. Thinking that he was going to punch Davenport, he followed him in planning to break up any fight. He saw and heard the shooting and after it he grabbed the killer by his collar saying: 'Come, Devey, this game will never do.' Devey then threw his guns in the street gutter. George Leeson picked up one and another passer-by, James Webb, picked up the other. Devey took the chance to attempt suicide and cut his own throat with a shoemaker's knife. The knife severed the windpipe but before he could finish himself off James Webb grabbed him by the arms, Leeson having been swept aside by a 'crowd of persons' who had rushed into the shop.

Both the victim's body and his live but injured killer were taken to hospital. Mr Bindley, the hospital's house surgeon, quickly diagnosed that the victim had died instantly. William Devey was treated and recovered from his wounds, no major blood vessels having been cut. Shortly after his admission Devey gave Bindley an envelope from his pocket which contained £3. 11s. 9d, a key, two small bills and a note on which was written: 'Call a sale immediately for the benefit of my wife and child. The lower premises for my creditors.' In Devey's pockets were found a new pistol bag, a pistol key and twenty-seven bullets.

On Thursday 5 April 1838, a Birmingham police officer, William Hall, received an anonymous letter which said that Richard Lawley, shoemaker, was also involved in a conspiracy against the victim and had supplied the knife with which the killer had attempted suicide. Lawley was arrested.

On Friday 6 April 1838, an inquest into the victim's death was held at the *White Swan* in Hospital Street. Samuel Farrington, George Leeson, James Webb, Emma Davis and her sister, Caroline Webley, Mr Bindley, Frederick Watson, Richard Lawley and William Hall gave evidence. They described the events outlined above.

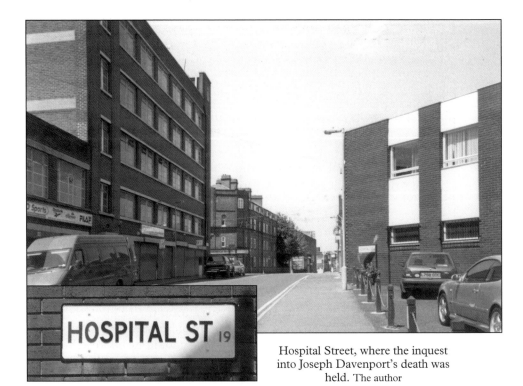

Hospital Street, where the inquest into Joseph Davenport's death was held. *The author*

Richard Lawley denied involvement in the murder, refused to answer most of the questions he was asked and denied that the shoemaker's knife that Devey had tried to kill himself with had been supplied by him. Richard Lawley was released and, having heard the evidence the coroner's jury, took just a minute to return a verdict that the victim had been murdered by William Devey who was committed to Warwick Gaol from where he made one failed escape bid.

The prisoner was brought to trial at the Warwick Summer Assizes on Thursday 9 August 1838. The judge was Mr Justice Bosanquet, Mr Sergeant Goulbourn and Mr Clarke were the prosecution counsel and Mr Hill and Mr Humfrey appeared for the defence.

The prosecution evidence was similar to that at the inquest though Benjamin Clulee also appeared. The defence accepted the facts of the case but claimed that the accused was insane having been tipped over the balance by his sufferings which he wrongly blamed on the victim.

Two of the accused's workers and two of his brothers-in-law

DREADFUL MURDER AND ATTEMPT AT SUICIDE.

On Wednesday evening, the neighbourhood of Snow-hill and Little Hampton-street was thrown into a state of great excitement by the perpetration of a most determined murder. It appears that for some time past an ill-feeling had existed between Mr. Joseph Davenport, landlord of the Pheasant, in Little Hampton-street, and a man named Wm. Devey, a plater. The latter suffering his hatred to beccme deadly, determined on destroying Mr. Davenport, and on the above day purchased a pair of pistols, loaded one of them, followed his victim to a shop in Snow-hill, and then shot him dead.

Yesterday, J. W. Whateley, Esq., coroner, held an inquest at the White Swan, Hospital-street. At three o'clock the following gentlemen were sworn on the jury:—Joseph Cartwright, foreman; John Shutt, Jeremiah Corbett, John Ward, Abraham Horton, Zechariah Parkes, William Finnimore, John Cook, John Rabone, William Hall, Edward Smallwood, Benjamin Morris, John Chatwin, and Samuel Hutton.

The jury having inspected the body, returned to the room, when the coroner having very briefly addressed them, the examination of witnesses proceeded:—

Mr. Samuel Farrington, living at No. 2, Union Court, Lower Tower-street, Birmingham, locksmith: A little after seven o'clock on Wednesday evening, Joseph Davenport, the deceased, came into Mr. Batkin's shop, where I work, and asked if Mr. Batkin was within; I went to call Mr. Batkin out of the workshop, and left the deceased in the shop; there was nobody else in the shop when I went; I was away about one minute. Directly after I got back into the shop, Devey came into the shop, as he entered he went up to the deceased and said, " D—n your eyes

Report from the *Birmingham Journal*, 7 April 1838. Birmingham Library

testified to Devey having been of unsound mind. Several other witnesses supported this view. One was a metal caster who the accused had called to cast metal for him on Tuesday 3 April 1838, the day before the killing, when he had seven hundredweight of cast metal in stock, an ample supply. The others were surgeons, one of whom had treated Devey for delirium tremens (alcohol withdrawal symptoms) and another who had been asked by Devey to open him up to examine him when he had merely been suffering from a bad cough.

The defence suggested that anyone who seriously tried to commit suicide must be mad. Also, two of the prisoner's aunts and a first cousin had died insane and a sister had tried to kill herself 'once or twice' before her marriage. To counter this evidence the prosecution recalled some of their witnesses who knew the prisoner and testified to his sanity. The defence retaliated that the best witnesses as to the state of his mind were his family and workers rather than casual acquaintances.

The judge then summed up. The jury took only a few minutes to convict William Devey of murder and he was sentenced to death. As he awaited execution he was questioned about the murder. He denied any memory of it but was a model prisoner who seemed thoroughly repentant. There was a petition got up in Birmingham for him to be pardoned but it was rejected and he was hanged outside Warwick Gaol on Thursday 23 August 1838. He died bravely.

The *Pheasant* disappeared not long after the above events, perhaps as a result. Little Hampton Street has disappeared though there is still a Great Hampton Street and a Hampton Street in the same area. The *White Swan* in Hospital Street survived until the 1890s, many other Birmingham pubs bearing that or similar names. The *Salutation* on Snow Hill survived until 1969 when it was swept away to make room for the inner ring road.

CHAPTER 10

The Shooting

Spernall, Alcester, 1842

Spernall is a small dispersed settlement about four miles north of Alcester. The whole parish covers slightly more than one and a half square miles. In 1841 it contained twenty-two houses and 107 people. One inhabitant was William Crowley, a well-to-do tenant farmer whose landlord was Sir Robert Throckmorton of Coughton Court.

William Crowley had been married twice, his second wife still living in 1842. He had children by both marriages. There was insanity in the family. By the first marriage, one daughter, Sarah, had first been confined in Henley in Arden Lunatic Asylum and then in another. Other children of this marriage were also insane including two other daughters and a son, John, who had once tried to stab himself.

By the second marriage there were two children. A daughter, Maria, was insane and a son, James Crowley, who was twenty-eight in 1842, appears from subsequent events to have been a paranoid schizophrenic.

Predictably, the family was rife with internal tensions. James Crowley accused his father of partiality towards his other children. James had had a good education and had used it to produce and distribute a pamphlet in 1841 outlining how his father had allegedly ill-treated him! The father, in contrast, took the view that his son was 'violent, dissipated, extravagant and undutiful'.

James Crowley had been ordered out of the family's farmhouse and had taken lodgings with a blacksmith about 300 yards away from his home. The father gave James, who was unemployed, an allowance of £50 a year (c.£10,000 today), together with a riding horse and its keep, on condition that he kept away from the family home.

James Crowley had several times threatened to kill his father and a frightened William Crowley had gone to the local magistrates. One of James's older half-brothers, Joseph Crowley, who lived nearby, was sworn in as a special constable and a twenty-year-old farmhand employee of the Crowley family, William

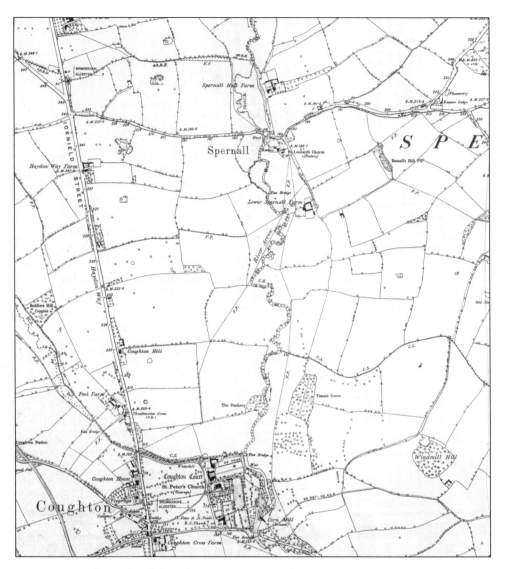

Spernall and Coughton area in c.1880, OS 6 inch to 1 mile map.
Ordnance Survey

Tilsley, who was married with two children, and who was six feet tall and built to match, was sworn in as his deputy.

On Thursday 22 December 1842, James Crowley came to his father's house and 'made use of very bad language' towards his father, having demanded and been refused extra money. The next day William Crowley sent Tilsley to warn him against returning to the farmhouse. Shortly after Tilsley returned, James, having ignored this warning, came again but having been ordered to go away went quietly.

At between eight and nine in the morning on Christmas Day 1842, James Crowley, wearing old clothes, came to his father's home again. His father again ordered his son away and, according to his father, James 'abused me with very foul language . . . and, thrusting his hand into a pocket as if in search of a pistol said he would shoot me.' The father, seeing no pistol, taunted his son, saying: 'Here I am, shoot away.' Tilsley was present and said to James: 'You had better leave him alone; you had better be quiet.' The son retorted: 'I will see you another day about this, old gentleman' and left.

William Crowley's second wife, James' mother, followed him into the fields. He said: 'Tell the old b...... to meet me in the fields in three quarters of an hour.'

About half past twelve in the afternoon that Christmas Day Mrs Crowley saw her son coming across the fields in his best

The largely Tudor Coughton Court where James Crowley's landlords, the Throckmortons, have lived since the fifteenth century. The author

clothes. She forced her husband to go upstairs. Henry Crowley, a half-brother of James Crowley, was in the house but was upstairs. Henry was a Liverpool shopkeeper and trader but was visiting his family home at Christmas.

On reaching his former family home, James Crowley fired a shotgun into the kitchen, breaking the window. William Tilsley, Joseph Street (who also worked for William Crowley) and fourteen-year-old John Nicholls, another employee, went out to confront James Crowley. Tilsley, Street and Nicholls saw 'James Crowley, master's son, opposite the window with a gun in his hand'. He said: 'What you're coming, are you?' James Crowley then cocked his gun, pointed it at Tilsley and fired. William Tilsley was hit in the head and his brains were literally blown out, leaving his wife a widow and his two children fatherless on Christmas Day. James Crowley then fled.

The victim's stunned companions got help and the body was carried into a wooden outhouse. Mr Morris, a Studley surgeon, was summoned and arrived at four in the afternoon. He looked at the body and found that a small lead bullet had gone in through the left eye and out through the back of the head, being stopped by the hat.

The police were called and John Findon, the Alcester Parish Constable, arrived. He went to James Crowley's cottage to find that he had fled, leaving behind a pistol. A shotgun, presumably the murder weapon, was found outside William Crowley's premises, one barrel of which had been fired, and another of which was loaded with powder and two bullets, the killer having presumably reloaded after the first shot.

Despite the absence of the killer an inquest into the victim's death was opened by Mr Hunt, the Warwickshire coroner, on Tuesday 27 December 1842 at the *Marlborough Head Inn,* in Studley, a large village near Spernall. Joseph Street, John Nicholls, Surgeon Morris and Henry and William Crowley gave evidence. The inquest returned a verdict that Special Constable Tilsley had been murdered by James Crowley.

A hunt was mounted for James Crowley but he appeared to vanish into thin air. In fact he had fled to the USA. With the frontier still open, America was then a much more open society than England, but it was also a country in economic depression and rent with the sectional divisions that were to lead to the Civil War. It was a bad country for even the honest poor and a terrible country for paranoid psychotics who imagined that the world owed them a living.

In 1844 James Crowley returned to England calling himself Mr

Smith. By this time William Crowley had died. The police learnt that James Crowley was in Chester, apparently because he had attempted to make contact with his family to find out about the situation at home. On 13 December 1844, Thomas Taylor, a Stratford-upon-Avon police officer, and a colleague, Joseph Lee, went to Chester in search of the accused. Having failed to find him at the *Black Dog* they found him at the *Castle and Falcon*. Lee seized the accused's arm saying: 'You may consider yourself a prisoner.' Taylor and Lee searched the prisoner, finding a double-barrelled pistol and a bullet mould.

As the prisoner was being searched a woman came in and the accused said to her: 'I shall be hung – I shot a man. I did no more than I would do tomorrow – I did my duty.' The prisoner repeated his confession before the Chester magistrates and signed a written statement which was witnessed by Mr Murrell, an assistant clerk to the Chester magistrates.

James Crowley was brought to trial at the Warwick Lent Assizes on Friday 4 April 1845. The judge was Mr Justice Maule, Mr Humfrey QC and Mr Mellor conducted the prosecution and Mr Hill QC and Mr Gale defended the prisoner. After an opening speech by Mr Humfrey the prosecution produced its witnesses. Joseph Street, John Nicholls and Surgeon Morris gave their evidence as at the inquest. William Crowley was dead and Henry Crowley was absent but to compensate for their absence the defence produced other witnesses. William Hobdale, who was a labourer for William Crowley, had seen the shooting. Earlier that day James Crowley had said to Hobdale that he would 'serve 'em out – there and then'. Thomas Rammell, another Spernall villager, testified that he had seen the prisoner in the vicinity of the murder scene on the day of the murder and had heard the gunshots. The Studley policeman John Findon also gave evidence. Thomas Taylor described the prisoner's arrest. The defendant's confession was corroborated by Mr Murrell, the Assistant Clerk to the Chester magistrates.

The prosecution had produced eight witnesses and could have produced more but decided that it had proved its case. The defence opened by calling Joseph Crowley, one of James's half-brothers, as a witness. He testified to the family's history of insanity. Mr Hill then made a long and emotive speech to the jury in which he pleaded with them to acquit the prisoner as insane. Having done so, he produced eleven favourable character witnesses for the defendant.

The jury took only two minutes to convict James Crowley of murdering William Tilsley and the judge sentenced him to death.

James Crowley was undoubtedly insane and after the trial evidence emerged that insanity was rampant in both his male and female ancestral lines. There was a petition and campaign for him to be pardoned but the Home Secretary, Sir James Graham, rejected all these appeals

James Crowley was hanged outside Warwick Gaol on Friday 18 April 1845, aged thirty-one. He seemed repentant of his crime and died bravely, even warning the hangman that the rope was overlapping his chin. The condemned man had been given the then usual glass of wine before his execution which was watched by a crowd of some 2,000 people, including many children.

Spernall's Anglican Church of St Leonard's has a medieval nave but its chancel was rebuilt in Victorian style in 1844, two years after the murder of William Tilsley. William Crowley's landlord Sir Robert Throckmorton's home of Coughton Court, which is a sixteenth century building, is today owned by the National Trust but the Throckmortons still live there, as they have done

Spernall's medieval church whose chancel was built in 1844 while James Crowley was still 'on the run'. The author

since the early fifteenth century. Their most famous member was Francis Throckmorton (1554–1584) who was tortured and executed after being convicted of being part of a plot to assassinate Queen Elizabeth I and bring Mary Queen of Scots to the throne.

CHAPTER 11

Just Thirteen

Coventry, 1844

In 1844 Coventry was a city with many pubs. One was the *Canal Tavern* in Leicester Row. As the accompanying plan from the *Coventry Herald* of 26 April 1844 shows, its ground floor consisted of a central passage leading from the front door to the back door which led into a back yard, accessible by two entries. At the front of the pub, on the ground floor, was a bar and a front kitchen which were entered by opposite doors from the central passage. At the back were the family's parlour and a back kitchen which were also entered by opposite doors from the central passage. The bedrooms were upstairs.

The *Canal Tavern* was kept by a married couple, Robert and Susan Golsby. They had three daughters: Ann, aged nine, Mary aged four and Emma aged seventeen months. To help look after them they had employed for about a year a thirteen-year-old 'sharp and intelligent' Kenilworth girl, Susannah Jarvis, as a nursemaid. They also had one other servant/employee – the terms were then interchangeable as they still are in legal terms – Maria Fowkes.

On Friday 19 April 1844 Susannah Jarvis took baby Emma for a walk. They returned about seven in the evening, and Susannah undressed Emma and put her in the cradle to sleep. Shortly afterwards Emma burst into tears. Susan Golsby went to comfort her baby and noticed several scratch marks on her neck which looked as if they had been made by finger nails. Once early in her employment Susannah Jarvis had shaken the baby but she had been rebuked and had not done so again.

On Saturday 20 April Emma was very reluctant to be taken out by Susannah Jarvis. Baby Emma was therefore looked after by Maria Fowkes while Susannah did other work.

Susan Golsby decided to dismiss Susannah. On Monday 22 April 1844 she gave Maria Fowkes, in Susannah's presence, a message to take to Susannah's parents that on Wednesday 24

North Coventry in c.1914, 25 inch to 1 mile OS map. Ordnance Survey

April 1844 she would be dismissed. Mrs Golsby explained in her message that Emma had taken a dislike to Susannah but said that it was possible that she might re-employ her later.

At between seven and eight in the evening on Monday 22 April 1844 Susan Golsby put Emma in her back kitchen cradle and went upstairs to take four-year-old Mary to bed, leaving nine-year-old Ann, who she had given a cake, to run the bar. Robert Golsby was out on business. After she had been upstairs for about four minutes Susan Golsby heard a 'cry of anguish or distress' and called: 'What is the matter?' Receiving no reply, she ran downstairs to hear Susannah Jarvis shout: 'A man has killed . . . the

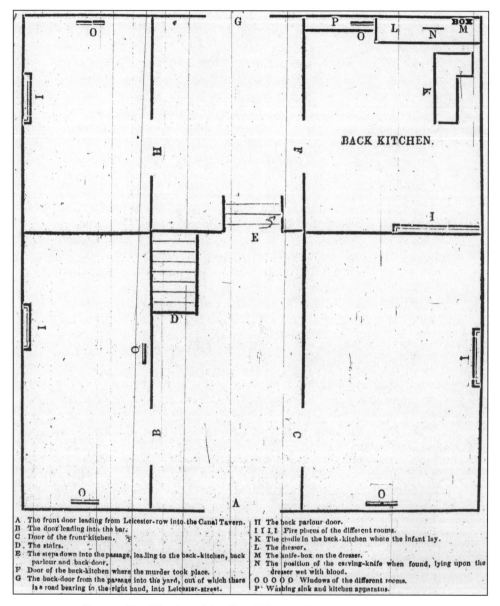

A . The front door leading from Leicester-row into the Canal Tavern.
B . The door leading into the bar.
C . Door of the front kitchen.
D . The stairs.
E . The steps down into the passage, leading to the back-kitchen, back parlour and back-door.
F . Door of the back-kitchen where the murder took place.
G . The back-door from the passage into the yard, out of which there is a road bearing to the right hand, into Leicester-street.

H . The back parlour door.
I I I I . Fire places of the different rooms.
K . The cradle in the back-kitchen where the infant lay.
L . The dresser.
M . The knife-box on the dresser.
N . The position of the carving-knife when found, lying upon the dresser wet with blood.
O O O O O . Windows of the different rooms.
P . Washing sink and kitchen apparatus.

Coventry Herald's plan of the *Canal Tavern*, 1844. Birmingham Library

baby!' Susan Golsby rushed into the kitchen, meeting Susannah, who came out 'somewhat agitated' and rubbing her hands on her dress. Susannah repeated her statement and Susan Golsby asked where the man had gone. Susannah replied: 'Down the Yard', to be told by the distressed mother that: 'No its no man – Its you I no doubt.' Susannah fled to the bar.

Susan Golsby went to the cradle to find that Emma had been stabbed and was covered in blood. The terrified mother ran with her dead baby to the front door of the pub and called out: 'Murder!' First, several passers-by came to her help and, at about eight that evening, a surgeon, John Overton, arrived and examined the dead baby's injuries. Emma had been stabbed in the breast, probably with one of the Golsbys' own carving knives. The wound had severed the jugular vein and penetrated the lungs. A bloodstained carving knife had been found on the back kitchen dresser and had been handed to Surgeon Overton by two of the passers-by, John Griffin and William Valentine, who had responded to the baby's mother's screams.

The police arrived and Surgeon Overton gave PC Salmon the bloodstained knife which was identified as a knife belonging to the Golsbys that had been left in a knife box on top of the back kitchen dresser that day, though it was usually kept in a drawer. PC Salmon found other bloodstains on the head of the cradle, the wall by its head and a few on the ground. The baby's pillow was saturated with blood. Susannah Jarvis was accused of the murder by the grieving mother and was called into the back kitchen. She denied the accusation but on the orders of Police Inspector Vice she was arrested and cautioned.

Susannah Jarvis said that while her mistress was upstairs she had gone out into the back yard privy. On returning she met a man coming out of the back door with blood on his hands and feet. He was a tall man and was wearing neither shoes nor stockings.

The Coventry Chief Constable, Mr Prosser, noticed that while the prisoner's hands were clean her pinafore and frock were bloodstained. She claimed that the blood spots on her pinafore were caused by her leaning against the back kitchen dresser while those on her frock were caused by her having fallen down in the passage. However, there were no bloodstains on the front of the dresser though there were on its top where the knife had been put down. Neither were there any bloodstains in the passage.

An inquest into Emma Golsby's death was opened at the *Wheel Tavern* in Leicester Row at four in the afternoon on Tuesday 23 April 1844. The jury consisted: of Mr Odell Senior, (foreman),

R Booth Esq, Mr Matthews (a plasterer), Mr Collins (a clothier), Mr Camwell (a wheelwright), Mr Anstey (a grocer), Mr Stone (a tailor), Mr Leigh (a baker), Mr Dickison (a hatter), Mr Taylor (a builder), Mr Hatchett (a baker), Mr Mark Spencer (a silk-man) and Mr R Francis (a boot-maker).

The first witness was the victim's mother who outlined the events above. Nine-year-old Ann Golsby denied that any such man as the prisoner described had entered the house, though she admitted that she had seen the accused go out to the back privy. Ann Golsby also denied that it had been she who had been the murderess as part of a game of 'pig-sticking'. She denied having ever taken part in such a game in her life. Surgeon Overton, PC Salmon, Inspector Vice and Chief Constable Prosser then gave evidence.

The inquest lasted two days, being resumed at four in the afternoon on Wednesday 24 April, having been adjourned to give the jury time to meet their work commitments. On the second day of the inquest, Mr Morris, a Coventry solicitor who was watching it on behalf of the prisoner's parents, who had been advised by the prosecution lawyers to hire a lawyer, produced two witnesses. A Mrs Ann Watson of Tower Street and Thomas King of Tower Street testified to having seen a man in the area on the evening of the murder, similar to the person described by the accused.

Nevertheless, the inquest returned a verdict that Emma Golsby had been murdered by Susannah Jarvis. She seemed calm but defiant and protested her innocence. Her panic-stricken parents shouted to her to refuse any food or drink and to starve herself to death rather than face the gallows, but she ignored this advice.

Fourteen-year-old Susannah Jarvis was brought to trial at the Coventry Summer Assizes on Tuesday 6 August 1844. The judge was Mr Justice Coltman, the prosecution counsel were Mr Mellor and Mr Adams and the defence was conducted by Mr Humfrey and Mr Miller.

The trial opened at nine in the morning and the first prosecution witness was Susan Golsby, the baby's mother. Her evidence was interrupted by the testimony of Mr Joseph Nevill, a surveyor, who produced in court a plan of the *Canal Tavern* and its surroundings. The third witness was Ann Golsby who testified as before.

Thomas Palmer then testified as to being among those who had come to the *Canal Tavern's* front door in response to Susan Golsby's screams. John Griffin told the court that he had been standing at his front door in Leicester Row when the alarm was given. He could see the back way to the *Canal Tavern* but had not seen anyone come in or go out, though he had not been taking much notice.

PC Salmon then gave evidence. As well as repeating his inquest evidence, he admitted that a man without shoes and stockings had been seen in the neighbourhood. The surgeon Mr Overton then repeated his earlier evidence and Mary Poole and Sarah Green, neighbours of Mrs Golsby's who had come to assist, then gave evidence which corroborated her testimony. After these witnesses had been heard, PC Salmon resumed his testimony. He described the bloodstains and how he had called the prisoner from the bar into the back kitchen on Mr Overton's advice. The accused had denied the murder, he said.

Inspector Vice then testified. He described the accused's story and said that he had found no bloodstains in the back passage or back yard, a fact which went against her claims. He made a search through the lodging houses for the shoeless and stockingless person she described and found that a 'miserable fiddler named Jones or Davis' had been found who matched her description. A Foleshill man, he was an alcoholic who had often been before the magistrates. He was produced in court and, predictably, denied any involvement in the murder.

Chief Constable Prosser was the next witness. He produced in court the prisoner's bloodstained frock and pinafore.

William Maddocks Underhill of Leicester Row gave evidence that on the night of the murder he had been waiting for his wife to come home, and had been walking backwards and forwards in front of his own house and past the two entries leading to the back of the *Canal Tavern*. He had been pacing up and down for more than a quarter of an hour before he heard the cry of 'Murder!' He had not seen any such man as the prisoner had described. John Townsend, Ann Lacy and Davis Jones, who had all been in the area at the time, also denied having seen such a person.

The prosecution had produced fifteen witnesses and announced that it had made its case. Mr Humfrey then spoke for the defence. He pointed out that the defendant was just fourteen and had only been thirteen at the time of the murder. She had no motive. The scratches that the victim's mother had noticed on baby Emma on the Friday before the murder might have been caused by pins, while the bloodstains on the defendant's frock and pinafore could have been caused by her coming into contact with 'something or somebody during the excitement upon the occurrence'. Mr Humfrey argued that the culprit was probably the shoeless and stockingless man described by the prisoner.

Five witnesses: Ann Watson, Mrs Harvey, Thomas King,

William Carter and Thomas Glenn testified to having seen such a man in the area of the murder, on the night of the murder and at about the right time.

Two witnesses, the Reverend Mr Parry, Vicar of Kenilworth, and Mrs Swaine, the schoolmistress at Kenilworth National School, gave character evidence. They described the accused as a kind girl.

Mr Mellor then replied for the prosecution. He said that he would be as glad as anyone else if (Susannah) Jarvis should turn out to be innocent but went over the evidence and pointed out that the 'poor, miserable beggar' who the defence 'insinuated' was guilty had no motive whatsoever for such a murder.

The judge then summed up. Although he was personally sympathetic to the prisoner, he inevitably stressed the strength of the evidence against her and the improbability of her account of events. He explained that children under seven were beyond the reach of the criminal law. Seven to thirteen-year-olds could only be prosecuted if it could be proved that they knew they were doing wrong. Fourteen-year-olds would have to face the full weight of the criminal law.

The jury retired at twenty-five to six in the evening. At half-past seven that evening, having been without refreshment for ten and a half hours, they requested some water but were refused. After sitting all night without a fire or candle, they were given bread and water at half past six on the morning of Wednesday 7 August. At ten o'clock that morning the court reopened and the jury reported that they had failed to reach a verdict. They were discharged and Jarvis was remanded in custody until the next assizes.

At the Coventry Winter Assizes, on Monday 2 December 1844, it was explained that the prisoner's defence counsel were unavoidably absent on other vital business. Consequently, the prosecution and the judge, Mr Justice Patteson, agreed to her being remanded in custody again.

Susannah Jarvis was brought to trial again at the Coventry Lent Assizes on Thursday 27 March 1844. The judge this time was Mr Justice Maule, the prosecution counsel were the same as at the first trial and the defence counsel were Mr Humfrey, as before, and Mr Mills, who replaced Mr Miller.

An ingenious model of the *Canal Tavern* and its surrounding area was produced in court. Seven prosecution witnesses: Susan Golsby, ten-year-old Ann Golsby, Mr Overton, PC Salmon, Inspector Vice, Chief Constable Prosser and William Maddocks Underhill, testified as at the first trial.

The defence produced eight witnesses. Ann Watson, Elizabeth

Harvey, Thomas King and Elizabeth Davis testified to having seen such a man as the prisoner described in the area of the murder, on its date and at the approximate time. William Good, who had been looking for a lost dog, testified that he had actually seen such a man coming out of the *Canal Tavern* back entry at the appropriate time and date and his evidence was corroborated by George Atkins. Both Good and Atkins denied having heard any cries of 'murder' which aroused the scepticism of the prosecution. The Reverend Parry and Mrs Swaine gave the accused a favourable character witness, as before.

The prosecution counsel, Mr Mellor, pointed out the narrow time frame in which the man the prisoner described would have had to commit such a murder. However, the judge, in a long summing up, pointed out the comparative weakness of the prosecution case and the strength of the defence case and this time the jury took only twenty minutes to acquit the prisoner.

Did Susannah Jarvis murder seventeen-month-old Emma Golsby out of resentment at being sacked? Did a beggar cum fiddler and petty thief sneak into the back of the *Canal Tavern* while its mistress was upstairs and the nursemaid at the privy and then silence a screaming baby with a handy carving knife? Or was the culprit nine-year-old Ann Golsby, as a widespread contemporary rumour claimed? I am sure, though, that if I had been around at the time, had any children and needed a nursemaid I would not have employed Susannah Jarvis after she was released from ten months in Coventry Gaol.

The *Old Wheel Tavern* where the inquest was held dated back to at least 1754. It closed in February 1932. The *Canal Tavern* where the murder happened survived the Second World War bombing of Coventry only to fall victim to postwar redevelopment and closed in 1963.

CHAPTER 12

The Poisoner

Nuneaton, 1849

uneaton is a north-east Warwickshire industrial town. In May 1849 two of its inhabitants were a married couple, Thomas and Mary Ball. Thomas was a weaver and was twenty-seven and Mary was thirty-one. They had been married for twelve years, the age of consent then being fourteen for men and twelve for women. They had a two-year-old daughter, five other children having died. The marriage had for some years been seemingly a happy one but by May 1849 it was in trouble. Thomas Ball strongly suspected his wife of having an affair with William Bacon, his employer's son. In reprisal he had beaten up his wife who had vowed revenge.

On Friday 18 May 1849, Thomas Ball went out fishing with two friends, Joseph Petty and Thomas Watts, on the Burton Canal, about four miles from Nuneaton. While they were out Thomas Ball felt thirsty and had some water from a pump. Shortly after he arrived home that evening he fell ill. Despite medical help he died in the small hours on Sunday 20 May. Medical tests revealed that he had died of arsenic poisoning and suspicion fell on his wife. She was arrested and on Thursday 24 May 1849 a coroner's inquest returned a verdict that Thomas Ball had been murdered by his wife, Mary, who was committed for trial at the next Coventry Assizes.

Mary Ball was brought to trial at the Coventry Summer Assizes on Friday 27 July 1849. The judge was Sir John Taylor Coleridge, the prosecution counsel were Mr Heyes and Mr Mellor and the defence counsel were Mr Miller and Mr Dennistoun. Mr Heyes opened the prosecution case by outlining the evidence against the prisoner. The first prosecution witness was Joseph Petty, a ribbon weaver. He described how Ball had gone out fishing with the witness and Thomas Watts on Friday 18 May 1849, at which time the victim seemed to be in perfect health. They had eventually separated and Thomas Ball returned home on his own.

At six in the evening on Friday 18 May, Mary Ball visited Petty and said: 'Tom's very ill; I want him to have a doctor but he won't.' The next morning she came and asked Petty to see her husband again for he was still very ill. He could not pass urine, his bowels were painful, and he felt very sick. He was convinced that he was dying and restlessly paced around his room. The witness stayed with his friend for about a quarter of an hour.

Joseph Petty visited the victim again at seven on the evening of Saturday 19 May when he 'was sick, purged and in pain'. The doctor had been. At twelve that night Petty visited his friend again to find that his arms were numb and cold. Petty rubbed his friend's arms.

At two in the morning on Sunday 20 May, Mary Ball came to Joseph Petty's house to tell him that her husband was dead. She cried and fainted but was revived and Petty and Mary Ball went to the victim's house and laid his body out.

In cross-examination Petty testified that the prisoner was prone to fainting attacks and had a very bad memory. Her fainting attacks were an especial problem when she was 'put about' (under stress). Nevertheless, they may not have entirely been an attention seeking strategy, for real epileptics sometimes semi-consciously have fits at convenient times and this is also a problem with the victims of nervous tics such as those caused by hydrocephalus.

The next witness was John Prouse, a surgeon who worked for the Nuneaton Poor Law Union. At the request of Mary Ball Prouse visited Thomas Ball on the afternoon of Saturday 19 May. He found the victim in bed complaining of stomach pains, bowel pain, sickness and thirst. He was also vomiting. Prouse prescribed pain killers, a purgative and pills to stop the vomiting.

At seven on the Saturday evening, Mary Ball visited Prouse again. She said that her husband was somewhat better, the vomiting having ceased. Prouse refused to come out again but at nine on Sunday morning Mary Ball came to him and told him that her husband was dead.

On the morning of Tuesday 22 May 1849, Prouse did a post-mortem on the victim's body. He diagnosed arsenic poisoning and sent the victim's stomach, stomach fluid, and part of the small intestines to George Shaw, Professor of Chemistry at Queen's College, Birmingham.

Professor Shaw was the third witness. He revealed that he had found about two or three grains of arsenic in the victim's remains and that this was probably only a small part of the arsenic that the victim had consumed.

The next witness was Selina Ryland the wife of Edward Ryland of Nuneaton. She knew the deceased and his wife and was friends

Nuneaton's medieval church, one of the few surviving buildings that Mary Bell would recognise today. The author

with them. About six weeks before the victim died Selina was told by Mary Ball that she had been beaten by her husband because of 'some lies which his sister Jane had told about her'. Selina challenged Thomas Ball about this to be told that he had seen enough through the 'chamber boards' to know that his wife had been having sex with William Bacon, aged twenty, whose father was Thomas Balls' employer.

Another time, in the spring of 1848, Thomas Ball had been going to Macclesfield to get work. The Balls breakfasted with the Rylands and Mrs Ryland gave Thomas some pork. He took his neckerchief off to tie it up with and asked his wife to fetch another. She refused and swore and he said that he would go without one. Mary Ball then said that she hoped that a train would run over her husband and that if he ever returned she would poison him.

Mary Bishop, the wife of Samuel Bishop, of Nuneaton, who lived two doors from the victim's father, a beer-house keeper, said that in March 1849 the prisoner and her cousin, a Mr Ward, had visited the Bishops. Mary Ball wished aloud that her husband and his family were all 'in hell' because of their jealously towards her, and said that the next time anything was said about her alleged affair she would murder her husband. Mary Bishop warned Mary Ball that this would mean death for her as well and the prisoner retorted that 'she would if she went to hell'.

The sixth witness was Elizabeth Richardson, the wife of Joseph Richardson, another neighbour of the Balls. On 4 May 1849, Mary Ball had asked Mrs Richardson to go with her and buy a pennyworth of arsenic (c. £1 in modern money) to kill bugs. That afternoon the two women went to Mr Ilife's druggist's (chemist's) shop. Mary Ball stayed outside the shop and her friend bought the arsenic which was wrapped up in two papers with big letters spelling 'Poison' on them. Mary asked her friend if the amount of arsenic she had purchased would be enough to kill someone with and was told: 'Yes, Mary, half that would.' Mary Ball asked her friend not to say anything about this purchase in case it caused trouble with the victim's family. The victim's sisters apparently believed that only dirty people's houses had bugs. Mary Ball rewarded her friend with a penny and a farthing – the price of half a pint of ale – which she suggested her friend buy herself.

On the Sunday morning after the victim died, the witness visited the new widow who seemed pleased that her husband had died. The witness reported the buying of the poison to Abel Vernon, the Constable of Nuneaton, and the Mary Ball claimed that she had used all the arsenic to kill bedbugs.

The next witness was Abel Vernon, the Nuneaton Constable. Having learnt about the arsenic purchase from the previous witness, he challenged the suspect about it. Mary Ball claimed to have used it all. However, on Monday 21 May the prisoner changed her story saying that she had put some of the arsenic on a pantry shelf and that the victim had taken it by mistake, thinking that it was stomach salts. She admitted to lying but said that she had done so through fear.

Ann Hopkins, a Nuneaton woman, and a friend of the deceased from childhood, described how, on Monday 21 May 1849, the prisoner had allegedly confessed to her that she had poisoned her husband saying that a post-mortem on the victim would mean that 'I shall be hanged'.

Thomas Watts, a weaver, then corroborated Joseph Petty's evidence. He also said that the prisoner had confessed to him on Monday 21 May that she had poisoned her husband. The witness expressed a hope that William Bacon had nothing to do with it and she replied that Bacon was 'as innocent as a lamb'. Thomas Watts later saw Bacon talking to Mary Ball and warned him off in case the authorities arrest him too.

The tenth and last prosecution witness, John Woodhouse, another Nuneaton man, said that on Sunday 20 May, after her husband's death, the prisoner asked him if a post-mortem could be avoided. The witness said that he thought not and the suspect said she hoped that one could be avoided.

Surgeon Prouse was then briefly cross-examined again. He repeated that the deceased had died of arsenic poisoning.

The prosecution announced that it had closed its case. Mr Miller spoke on behalf of the defence. He said that the crudity of Mary Ball's threats to her husband meant little given 'the station of life in which the prisoner and her deceased husband moved', where such 'coarse language' was routine in contrast to higher and more 'refined' circles.

Mr Miller suggested that the deceased had accidentally taken arsenic in mistake for stomach salts. The prisoner had been reckless in putting arsenic on a pantry shelf but this would mean, at most, a manslaughter charge. She had indeed lied to Constable Vernon but this had been motivated by fear.

The judge then summed up. He pointed out that the defence's story was unlikely and that the absence of direct witnesses to the crime meant little, for no sane murderer would poison their victim with witnesses present.

The jury took two hours to convict the prisoner of murder, recommending that she be shown mercy. The judge asked on what grounds they made such a recommendation and after a minute's consultation the jury returned an unqualified guilty verdict. The judge then sentenced the accused to death.

After the trial the condemned woman continued to protest her innocence but great pressure was put on her to confess. On Thursday 2 August 1849 she saw her two-year-old daughter for the last time.

On Saturday 4 August 1849, at about half past five in the evening, while the Coventry Gaol governor, Mr Stanley, was on business in Birmingham, the prison chaplain, the Reverend Richard Chapman, visited the prisoner in her cell, in the presence of Miss Susanna Winter, the Assistant Matron. The Reverend Chapman held Mary Ball's hand over a lighted candle flame for about two minutes. She eventually managed to pull her hand away and the chaplain asked her if that hurt, what did she think the flames of hell would be like?

On hearing about this incident the prison governor arranged a hearing by the prison's visiting magistrates. Susanna Winter bravely testified as to what had happened and the Reverend Chapman was dismissed from his job.

On Sunday 5 August 1849 Mary Bell confessed to the murder. She gave as her motive her husband's repeated adulteries and that he had repeatedly beaten her. She had tricked her husband into thinking that the arsenic was stomach salts to give herself an alibi.

At just after ten in the morning on Thursday 9 August 1849 Mary Ball was hanged in front of Coventry Gaol. A 'quiet and orderly' crowd of more than 18,000 people watched the execution, the first in Coventry for eighteen years, the previous execution in Coventry having been that of nineteen-year-old Mary Ann Higgins in 1831 for poisoning her uncle.

Mary Ball was probably a murderess. She had a clear motive for killing her husband, she had bought poison and behaved suspiciously when she did so and she had certainly been reckless in putting arsenic on a pantry shelf. However, this might have been an innocent mistake given her health problems. Moreover, much of the evidence against her was flawed. For instance, was she really reckless enough to confess to murder to friends of her husband?

As for Mary's confession, her torture by the Reverend Chapman was an extreme case and he was promptly sacked, but it illustrates the obsession with getting a confession that throws light on the lesser but still fierce moral pressures that were used to obtain them. Such death cell confessions were widely publicised until the twentieth century when a blanket of secrecy was imposed on executions but even afterwards they were often leaked. This case shows how much they were often worth.

CHAPTER 13

The Trip to Birmingham

Rugby, 1854

Rugby is a mid-Warwickshire industrial town and typifies the Midlands combination of northern and southern social characteristics. On the one hand it houses the great public school of Rugby where Thomas Arnold was headmaster from 1828 to 1842, which inspired Thomas Hughes' novel *Tom Brown's Schooldays*, and where the game of rugby was invented. On the other hand, by 1854, Rugby was a great railway and industrial centre, the London to Birmingham Railway which passes through it having been

Rugby Railway Station today. The author

completed sixteen years earlier in 1838. In 1854, one Rugby resident employee of the London and North Western Railway Company was a thirty-eight-year-old railway policeman, William Voss. He had worked for the company for nine years and was for most of that time 'an honest and trustworthy servant'. He was five foot, eleven inches tall, and was of a 'dark complexion', with 'black curly hair', thus possibly being of what we would call mixed race.

William lived with his widowed mother Elizabeth Voss in a two-room, one-up, one-down cottage. The downstairs room was a kitchen-cum-living room and the upstairs a bedroom. A widower, William, had three sons who lived in London and three daughters. One daughter was a servant in Bristol. Another eighteen-year-old, Sarah Ann, his oldest daughter, a servant in Peterborough, was engaged to be married and was 'a very stupid child' i.e. she had what we would call borderline learning difficulties. A third daughter, Mary, was a servant in London.

William Voss developed syphilis and this affected his brain, causing his behaviour to become increasingly erratic. On 9 August 1854 the London and North Western Railway Company dismissed him. He looked for other work, even going to London from the 5th to the 21st of October 1854 but he could not hold a job down. He was extremely restless, suffered severe insomnia, imagined that people, including his own family, were plotting against him, and found any noise unbearable, even a clock ticking tormented him, while he found the noise of his mother opening her snuff box unbearable.

The slowly dying man was treated by a Rugby doctor, John Baker. The medical profession was still one in which a medieval surgeon would have felt at home. Dr Baker gave his patient various treatments,. mainly bleeding and treatment for his ulcerated syphilitic arm. The bleeding may have had some short term psychosomatic benefit but must have further weakened Voss.

William Voss was nursed by a near neighbour, Mrs Ann Godwin, the wife of labourer George Godwin. The Godwins had one son and lived about six doors away from William Voss and his mother.

Realising that he was dying, William Voss summoned his three daughters home. When he was well he had been a kind parent. The daughter who worked in Bristol decided to stay there but Sarah Ann returned from Peterborough and Mary from London giving up their servant jobs. Sarah Ann slept in the same bed as her grandmother Elizabeth, William Voss sleeping in another bed in the same room. Mary Voss slept in a neighbour's house but spent the rest of the day with her father and grandmother.

Although William still had some savings, they were running out. Sarah Ann and Mary planned to go to get work as servants in Birmingham. Mary had lived there before, as a trainee shoe binder, a job which she had found too much for her eyesight. She had lived in lodgings there before and was planning for her and her sister to use the same lodgings again. Their father was very hostile to this plan.

At ten in the morning on Saturday 18 November 1854, Ann Godwin visited the Voss house to see how William was. She was told that her patient had gone into Rugby town and Ann Godwin said: 'Then of course he's better.' As Mrs Godwin left, Elizabeth Voss came out into her yard and wrung her hands 'with every sign of deep affliction'. Mrs Godwin asked if Elizabeth had got bowel trouble, to be told that she had got 'the heart complaint'. She seemed about to tell Mrs Godwin something but Mary Voss said 'No, grandmother, not yet'. When Ann Godwin got back to her own home she said to her 'little boy': 'I don't know what's the matter at Mrs Voss's but there's something I'm sure.'

At about half past eleven that morning, Mary Voss came to Ann Godwin's house and said that her grandmother wanted to speak to her. Mary refused to say what had happened and Ann Godwin came to the Voss house where Elizabeth told her that her son, William, had murdered his daughter, Sarah Ann, who was lying dead in bed. William had fled having told his terrified family that he was going to give himself up to the Rugby police.

Ann Godwin summoned Dr Baker and the Rugby police. Dr Baker arrived at about half past twelve in the afternoon and examined the dead body. Sarah Ann Voss had been stabbed twice in the neck. One wound on the right side of the neck would have been survivable but the other wound had cut the jugular vein and had been fatal.

The police arrived at one in the afternoon under Super-intendent James Isaacs of the Knightlow Hundred Division of the Warwickshire Police, which included Rugby. He and his men looked for a murder weapon. They found a case knife in the bedroom, a razor inside a trunk which they broke open, and a pair of scissors with some tallow on them. They decided that none of these items was the murder weapon.

On Monday 20 November 1854, an inquest opened at the *Windmill Inn* in Rugby into the victim's death, even though William Voss was still on the run having lied when he said to his mother that he would hand himself in to the police.

The first witness was Elizabeth Voss, the suspect's mother and the victim's grandmother. On the night of Friday 17 November, William had gone to bed after having a slice of toast and a cup of cocoa. He had seemed no worse than before. At about ten that evening, Elizabeth heard her son pacing around in his bedroom and smoking. She warned him that smoking was unhealthy and he got into bed.

William Voss got up at about five in the morning, sat in a bedroom chair and turned off the fire. His mother asked him if he was too warm but he did not answer, instead pacing around the room. At about half six in the morning his mother got up and went downstairs to make breakfast. William came downstairs and said: 'Are you having breakfast already? Ann was getting up but I made her get into bed again.' Elizabeth then asked her son if he wanted breakfast and poured him a cup of tea. William then went back upstairs and asked Sarah Ann if she wanted a cup of tea but she did not answer.

Mary Voss then came in from the neighbour's house where she lodged. Elizabeth said to her: 'Your father has gone to lie down you had better not go upstairs but go if you like.' Mary went upstairs and came down crying saying that her father was 'talking harshly' to Sarah Ann.

Elizabeth Voss went out in the yard to do some washing and heard Sarah Ann crying. Thinking that William was whipping his daughter, she came in. At about a quarter past eight, William came downstairs and said to his mother: 'I have been talking to Ann about this trip to Birmingham but she won't speak to me.' He was told by his mother: 'Let her alone how you do worrit (sic)'. Mary Voss, then went upstairs where, as Elizabeth explained in response to an interjection by the coroner, she discovered the body. Elizabeth ran upstairs after Mary and said:'William don't hurt the poor child' but by this time William had done the murder.

Elizabeth Voss said to her son: 'Don't beat her William', but she did not see the murder though she heard a gurgling coming from her dying granddaughter's throat. The witness asked her son: 'You wicked child what have you done?' to be told: 'I have killed her and I shall be hanged for it.' Elizabeth said to her son: 'Don't blame me', to be told: 'There's nobody to blame but myself.' By this time it was half past eight. William's hands were blood stained but his mother did not see any murder weapon.

The murderer briefly returned upstairs and coming back down again fastened the bedroom door which was at the bottom of the stairs. He kissed his mother and his daughter Mary and said that he was going to Rugby to hand himself over to the police. He gave his mother his watch and purse, which contained two sovereigns – a sovereign was £1 and was worth perhaps £200 in modern money – and some silver money. He then made her and Mary swear on a prayer book, which he probably mistook for a New Testament, not to go to the police but to wait for them to arrive. At half past eleven Elizabeth Voss finally contacted Ann Godwin who called for a surgeon and the police.

Elizabeth Voss was asked about the murder weapon. She explained that the razor with which her son had shaved himself on the Friday morning before the murder was missing.

The second witness was Mary Voss. She explained that on the Friday night before the murder she had asked her father for permission for she and her sister to go to Birmingham but had been given no conclusive answer. Mary had challenged her sister Sarah Ann about rumours that Sarah Ann was pregnant or had had a child out of wedlock, but her sister had denied them.

Mary Voss had come to her grandmother's house at half eight on the morning of the murder and had asked her grandmother how her father was. Concerning the time discrepancy, with her mother's account of events, William Voss was in the habit of turning off clocks because he could not stand them ticking. Mary was told that he had gone back upstairs and was probably dozing. She went upstairs and met her father at the top of the stairs with a lighted candle in his hand. He blew it out and Mary kissed her father and said: 'Good Morning.'

William told Mary that he had been talking to Sarah Ann about her going to Birmingham and Sarah Ann said to her sister: 'You are as much in fault as me. Have you told father all that you can?' Sarah Ann apparently believed that Mary was trying to blame her for the plans to go to Birmingham. Mary came back downstairs and began to cry. William came down and said: 'Don't worry; it wasn't your fault, get your breakfast' and went back upstairs. Five minutes later, Mary heard her sister screaming. She ran upstairs and heard her sister's dying words: 'Oh father I'll never do so again.'

Mary saw her father kneeling on her sister's bed and pulled him off. He had a large pair of scissors in his hand and these slightly cut Mary. Elizabeth Voss then arrived and Mary corroborated her account of William's confession. William Voss then lit his pipe saying: 'I'll have a bit of bacca for the last time.' He came downstairs and drank some white wine and gave some to his mother and to his daughter, Mary. He burnt some letters, gave Mary a gold ring and his mother his watch and purse. He went back upstairs, pulled Sarah Ann's body up by her hair and covered her up with the bed clothes. At nine o'clock he left his house, having made Elizabeth and Mary swear not to go to the police.

The third inquest witness was Dr Baker who described the victim's wounds and William Voss's medical condition. The inquest was then adjourned until the next day to give Dr Baker time to do a post-mortem. The inquest resumed at six in the evening on Tuesday 21 May 1854, still at the *Windmill*. Dr Baker confirmed his earlier account of the victim's injuries, went into more detail about the suspect's mental health problems, and was able to deny that the victim had been pregnant or 'enciente' as he put it this being a Victorian euphemism for pregnant.

Ann Godwin and Superintendent Isaacs then testified the Superintendent reporting that William Voss was still on the run. The coroner summed up, saying that the identity of the murderer was clear and that they had insufficient evidence to decide if the accused was insane. The jury took only a few minutes to return a verdict that the victim had been murdered by her father and, in his absence, he was committed for trial at the next Warwick Assizes.

A manhunt had already been mounted. William Voss had gone alongside the Leamington Spa railway until he came to the Lawford footbridge which he crossed. He passed the Victoria Works and reached Lawford Heath. He then went towards Bourton and Leamington Hastings and went through Hill into the Rugby and Southam Turnpike Road to Birdingbury Wharf where he offered his waistcoat for sale. He reached Southam and turned towards Napton and Stockton. He was finally caught on Wednesday 22 November 1854 by a party of labourers in Stockton parish and handed over to Inspector Chamberlain of the Southam police. By this time the suspect had probably disposed of the murder weapon which was never identified.

The suspect was taken back to Rugby and was then sent to Warwick Gaol. He was brought to trial at the Warwick Lent Assizes on Monday 19 March 1855. The judge was Mr Justice Coleridge, Mr Spooner conducted the prosecution and Mr O'Brien the defence.

For the prosecution Elizabeth Voss and her granddaughter Mary Voss, Ann Godwin, Dr Baker and Superintendent Isaacs testified largely as before. Dr Baker made the prisoner's insanity clearer than he had at the inquest and the judge criticised him for not having been more forthcoming then. Inspector Chamberlain described the prisoner's arrest and how he had said: 'Voss I charge you with killing your eldest daughter by cutting her throat.' The arrested man replied: 'Did I Mr Chamberlain? I didn't as I know off. I have been bad lately – my head is so bad.'

The *Rugby Tavern*, formerly the *Windmill Inn* where the inquest into Sarah
Ann Voss's death was held in 1854. The author

The defence counsel, Mr O'Brien, pointed out that all the
evidence clearly showed that the defendant was insane. For
the defence, Dr William Henry Parsey, the doctor at Hatton
Lunatic Asylum near Warwick, testified that on 9 February 1855
and subsequently, he had examined the prisoner at the request of
the visiting magistrates. He found that he was insane.

The judge summed up laying great stress on Dr Parsey's
evidence. The jury took less than a minute to acquit the prisoner
due to insanity and William Voss was ordered to be detained at
Her Majesty's Pleasure.

Rugby remains a major railway centre though the direct line to
Leamington Spa fell victim to Dr Beeching's cuts last century.
The *Windmill Tavern* where the inquest was held still exists
though its name was late last century changed to the *Rugby
Tavern*. Syphilis remains a very dangerous disease but it is usually
curable with antibiotics and its final stage general paralysis of the

insane is rare, at least in countries with good medical services. Readers may mourn for an eighteen-year-old girl who was murdered by an insane father having loyally returned home to be with him at the last. However, the trial jury's verdict spared a mother and granddaughter from knowing that their evidence had sent their son and father to the gallows.

In 1857, two years after this trial, Thomas Hughes' classic *Tom Brown's Schooldays* was published. It describes life as a pupil at Rugby School in a world incredibly remote from that of this case yet one whose characters inhabited the same town.

CHAPTER 14

The Brawl

Fenny Compton, 1863

Even after the creation of proper police forces, villages carried on appointing their own amateur parish constables. Fenny Compton was and is a small south Warwickshire village and in 1863 its parish constable was a local farmer and butcher, Thomas Ricketts. In October 1863 his uncle, Charles Plummer, a sixty-seven-year-old retired Bascot Heath farmer, a resident of Broad Street, Warwick, and his

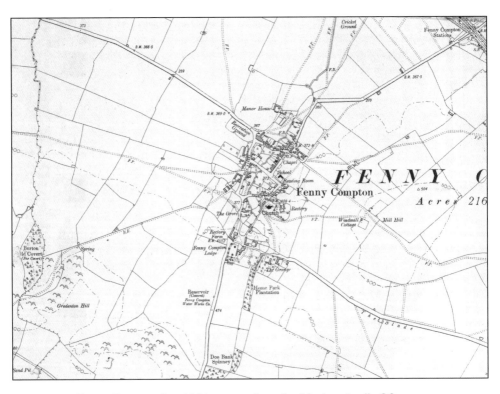

Fenny Compton in c.1906, extract from the 6 inch to 1 mile OS map.
Ordnance Survey

wife, were staying with their nephew Thomas Ricketts, who was married with at least one child.

On the evening of Sunday 18 October 1863, Thomas Ricketts and Charles Plummer, who was lame and walked with a stick, went out for a walk with Thomas's little terrier on the Ricketts' farm. As they were looking at some livestock, two labourers, twenty-one-year-old Charles Beere, and his eighteen-year-old brother Henry Beere, from North-end in Burton Dasset parish, who had been out drinking in the local pubs, came walking along the Fenny Compton to North-end footpath and met Ricketts and Plummer. The little terrier ran up to the Beere brothers. Although Ricketts later denied that the dog barked or tried to bite them the brothers swore at it. Thomas Ricketts protested and Charles Beere demanded to know who Ricketts was and what the dog was to do with him. Thomas Ricketts gave his name and said that he was the occupier of the field and the parish constable. He then said that if the Beere brothers did not 'go about their business' he would arrest them as drunk and disorderly.

Charles Beere took off his jacket and said that he would let Ricketts see if he was drunk and who was parish constable. He was about to strike Ricketts when Henry Beere grabbed his older brother and stood in front of him. Thomas repeated that he was the constable and that it would be wrong for Charles Beere to assault him.

Bursting from his brother's restraint, Charles Beere struck Ricketts with his clenched fist on the left of the head. Thomas took his uncle's walking stick out of his uncle's hands and knocked Charles Beere down with it, striking him several times on the ground. Charles Beere managed to get up but Ricketts knocked him down again. Henry Beere appealed to Rickets, saying: 'Don't hit him while he is down,' but Ricketts ignored him and carried on hitting Charles Beere, breaking his uncle's stick on him. Eventually, both Charles Beere and Ricketts ended up wrestling on the ground. Charles Plummer had kept out of the fight, but Henry Beere came to his brother Charles Beere's rescue and the two got the better of Ricketts.

Thomas Ricketts managed to break away from the Beere brothers and fled back to his farm to get help. Meanwhile, despite protests from his brother Henry, Charles Beere turned his drunken wrath on the helpless Charles Plummer, knocked him down and repeatedly kicked him in the head and chest.

Thomas Ricketts got back home and sent his second cousin and employee William Ricketts after the Beere brothers while Thomas went to fetch the local paid policeman, PC Oughton. William

Fenny Compton Church. The author

Ricketts got to the scene of the fight and saw the Beere brothers running away towards North-end. William found Charles Plummer lying badly hurt in a furrow. Blood was pouring from his head and William asked him if he was hurt, to be told that he was 'hurt very much indeed'.

PC Oughton arrived and Charles Plummer was taken back to the Ricketts' farmhouse and put to bed while PC Oughton and Thomas and William Ricketts pursued and arrested the Beere brothers. They were taken back to the Ricketts' farmhouse where the dying Charles Plummer identified Charles Beere as his assailant. Elizabeth Neale, the wife of a local shomaker, Thomas Neale, witnessed this statement.

On Monday 19 October 1863, two Fenny Compton surgeons, Thomas Ebbage and Thomas Elkington, visited Charles Plummer. His head injuries were horrific and his chest injuries included three broken ribs. Even a modern casualty unit would have found his injuries a major challenge and in 1863 his condition was hopeless. He died the next day and what had started out as a fight became a murder inquiry.

The Beere brothers had already been arrested and, after initially denying any involvement in the attack, they confessed both to PC Oughton and to Inspector Gaskins of the Southam police. Henry Beere blamed his older brother saying: 'You know Charles if you'd been ruled by me you wouldn't have kicked the old man and then we shouldn't have been here.' Charles Beere replied: 'I know that.'

On Wednesday 21 October 1863, at the *Red Lion* in Fenny Compton, the coroner, Mr W S Poole, opened an inquest into Charles Plummer's death. One dramatic moment was when one of Charles Beere's boots was examined in court and two of the victim's hairs were found on it. On Friday 23 October, after being once adjourned, the coroner's Jury returned a verdict that the victim had been murdered by Charles and Henry Beere.

The Beere brothers were tried for murder at the Warwickshire Winter Assizes on Friday 4 December 1863. The judge was Mr Baron Martin, the prosecution was conducted by Mr Bennett and the Honourable E C Leigh who were instructed by Mr E Poole of Southam, and the prisoners were defended by Mr Fitzstephen who was instructed by Mr J Lane of Stratford-upon-Avon.

Mr Bennett opened the prosecution case. He admitted that if it had been Thomas Ricketts who had been killed there would have been an element of provocation but the victim was an 'unoffending old man' who had been repeatedly kicked having taken no part in the earlier fight.

Thomas and William Ricketts, PC Oughton, Inspector Gaskins, and Surgeons Elkington and Ebbage gave their evidence. The judge ruled that Henry Beere had no case to answer.

Mr Fitzstephen spoke on behalf of Charles Beere, arguing that the case against his client should be reduced to a manslaughter charge. He argued that the prisoner had been drunk, and that Thomas Ricketts's officiousness and violence was partly responsible for what had happened.

The judge in his summing up ordered the jury to acquit Henry Beere. In contrast, he said that Charles Beere was clearly the killer and that the only question was whether his crime was murder or manslaughter. The judge went over the law as related to the difference between murder and manslaughter essentially saying that the case was on the border line.

The jury acquitted Henry Beere and he was released a free man, having spent six weeks in prison. Charles Beere was convicted of manslaughter and the judge sentenced him to life imprisonment with hard labour saying that it was one of the worst manslaughter cases he had ever encountered. The judge said that this case should teach people to stay away from pubs, especially on a Sunday. However, this was a society where even such solemn events as coroner's inquests were still held in pubs!

Fenny Compton remains a charming small Warwickshire village. The *Red Lion* still exists though it is today called the *Merrie Lion.*

CHAPTER 15

The Navigation Street Riot

Birmingham, 1875

B y 1875, Birmingham was a rapidly expanding, great industrial centre, proudly calling itself 'The City of a Thousand Trades' and the 'Workshop of the World'. Like any great city it had rough areas. In 1875, one of these areas was Navigation Street in the town centre, off which ran Fordrough Street, on which stood a public house, the *Bull's Head* whose landlord was George Cunnington.

Navigation Street today. The author

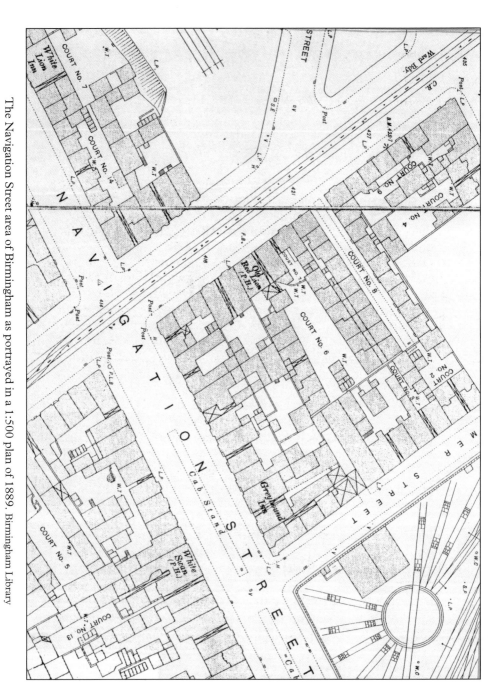

The Navigation Street area of Birmingham as portrayed in a 1:500 plan of 1889, Birmingham Library

On the night of Saturday 6 March 1875, two burglars used a ladder to climb up to and break into through a window George Cunnington's first floor bedroom at the *Bull's Head*. They stole a cashbox, a vest and a pair of trousers. During the burglary a pub employee, Sarah Ann Hyde, noticed that the light was on in the bedroom, looked in through the keyhole and saw two men. She recognised one as nineteen-year-old brass chandelier-maker William Downes, of Box Iron Yard, Fordrough Street. The other burglar later turned out to be nineteen-year-old canal boatman Thomas Carey.

The next day, Sarah Ann Hyde told George Cunnington what she had seen and he called the police. Police constables John Goodman and Charles Fletcher arrived in plain clothes, to find that Downes was drinking in the *Bull's Head* bar. At the landlord's request the bar was cleared and Downes was arrested for burglary.

Downes came quietly but a mob of 'some thirty or forty strong' objected to his arrest and followed the two plainclothesmen, throwing stones at them. The two officers asked for help from uniformed PC William Lines who was on duty at the corner of Fordrough and Navigation Streets. Lines was thirty, had been a policeman for eleven years, and was married with a daughter. PC Lines tried to control the mob and, seeing he was in trouble, the plainclothesmen sent the nearby uniformed Sergeant Joseph Fletcher, who had been on duty at the corner of Navigation and Suffolk streets, to help him.

PCs Goodman and Fletcher got Downes safely back to Moor Street Police Station but the mob attacked Sergeant Fletcher and PC Lines as they tried to hold it back and to arrest the participants. In the course of a riot in Navigation and Suffolk streets, Sergeant Fletcher was knocked to the ground and repeatedly kicked and PC Lines was stabbed under the left ear.

Sergeant Fletcher made a full recovery but PC Lines was mortally injured. On Saturday 20 March, as he lay dying in hospital, he made a deposition naming and identifying a twenty-three-year-old brass caster ,John Cresswell, a twenty-two-year-old iron bedstead maker, Aaron Rogers, and an eighteen-year-old stamper, Thomas Whalen, as being among his assailants. Rogers had said to Lines: 'Ah, we want to get you by yourself you . . . pig', an interesting early usage of this hostile slang term for a police officer. A fourth man who Lines could not identify had stabbed him.

A number of other men had been arrested and charged with rioting in the days after, including a twenty-year-old Irish Catholic iron worker called Jeremiah Corkery who was arrested three days later. He had a criminal record dating back to when he was ten and had been convicted of wounding but escaped prison because of his 'extreme youth'. He had later served nine prison terms on various charges including two sentences for assaulting a policeman, one of one month and another of two months.

PC Lines died on Wednesday 24 March 1875 and a riot case became a murder inquiry. Evidence from several witnesses named Jeremiah Corkery as having stabbed PC Lines and an inquest into the victim's death was opened at the Birmingham Public Office in Moor Street on Saturday 27 March 1875 by the coroner, Dr Birt Davies.

The first witness was PC Lines's widow, Elizabeth. Her husband had left home at half one in the afternoon on Sunday 7 March 1875, a healthy man. The next time she saw him he was lying in Birmingham's Queen's Hospital at half eleven that night with a knife wound under his left ear.

The next witness was PC John Goodman. On the night of Sunday 7 March, he and PC Fletcher had gone to the *Bull's Head* to arrest William Downes who came peacefully. However, Goodman heard a shout from behind: 'Don't let the .... take him.' PC Goodman then called to Lines to help him. The witness saw Sergeant Fletcher and said: 'For God's sake run up to Lines', because: 'I thought two would be better than one'. PCs Goodman and Fletcher took Downes to the police station and saw no more of the riot.

James Moore, a Fordrough Street umbrella-maker, told the inquest how, at about a quarter to nine on Sunday 7 March 1875, he had seen Sergeant Fletcher being kicked as he lay on the ground and saw PC Lines knock a rioter down with his truncheon before himself being stabbed in the ear by Corkery. The fourth witness, Walter Vernon, a Bull's Head Yard, Fordrough Street marble polisher, described having seen a policeman lying on the ground and being kicked and having seen PC Lines first strike Corkery in the face with his truncheon, and then being stabbed by Corkery.

A Fordrough Street button coverer, Mary Ann Conway, and Ann Whalen, a Fordrough Street umbrella wirer, also described seeing Corkery stab PC Lines in retaliation for being hit in the face with his truncheon. Ann Whalen was a sister of Thomas Whalen who was himself under arrest for alleged rioting, and who had been named by PC Lines as one of his assailants.

The seventh witness was Francis George Hamilton, resident surgeon at the Queen's Hospital. He explained that for ten days the victim had appeared to be recovering well but then a traumatic aneurism caused by his stab wound became apparent. Medical students used their fingers to 'digitally' compress the carotid artery for thirty-three hours and it briefly seemed to help. Eventually, an operation to ligature the carotid artery was performed by Surgeon Sampson 'Sam' Gamgee but the operation failed, the aneurism burst and the patient died.

After the medical evidence, Detective Constable Beard produced the dying man's deposition but the coroner ruled that it was irrelevant to the case since it did not name Corkery. The coroner summed up, describing the fatal knifing as wholly 'un-English', ruled that Corkery was clearly the killer, as four witnesses had testified, and that the victim had clearly died of his injury. Since the victim was a policeman, what might normally be manslaughter was murder unless a trial jury decided otherwise. Finally, the coroner gave Corkery the chance to speak.

Corkery said that on the evening of Saturday 6 March, having been out drinking, he had been mugged and robbed of his watch and chain in Price Street by three young men, and had been treated at the General Hospital that night. The next day, having recovered, he had been out drinking at a pub on Snow Hill at the time of the murder which he knew nothing about. The coroner's jury took ten minutes to return a verdict that PC Lines had been murdered by Corkery.

On Monday 29 March 1875, PC Lines was buried at Witton Cemetery which was then on the outskirts of Birmingham. Apart from the family, the mourners included the Birmingham Chief Constable, Mr Glossop, six superintendents, seven inspectors, twenty-one sergeants and 210 constables. The Birmingham Police Band played and a number of prominent local politicians also attended, including Aldermen Brinsley and Taylor.

A fund was set up to help the victim's widow and child. Donations were headed by £5 (c.£1,000 today) from the then Mayor of Birmingham, Joseph Chamberlain, Neville Chamberlain's father. £101 was eventually handed over to the widow and other money was put in trust for the child and for the widow's old age.

On Tuesday 30 March 1875, the Birmingham magistrates charged Corkery with murder separately to the inquest. Other persons allegedly concerned with the riot were also charged and Downes was charged with burglary. Carey was arrested on 1 April 1875 and charged with burglary the next day, having 'eluded' the police for more than three weeks.

The Warwick Summer Assizes opened on Thursday 8 July

1875. In his charge to the grand jury Mr Justice Field devoted much attention to the Corkery case, to the trial of seven other men accused of rioting, and to the trial of Downes and Carey for burglary. The grand jury returned true bills against all ten prisoners.

On Friday 9 July 1875, Corkery was tried for the murder of PC Lines. The judge was Mr Justice Field, the prosecution counsel were Mr Adams QC and Mr Dugdale, and the Honourable E C Leigh appeared for the defence. Mr Adams opened the prosecution case, explaining that murders of police on duty were rare and that 'the English had been described as a law loving people and until recently the inhabitants of the borough of Birmingham might have claimed to have a prominence in that respect as in many others. Unfortunately during the past few years a spirit of lawlessness and insubordination had arisen. Policemen had again and again been assaulted, sometimes seriously, and at last the outrages had culminated in the death of the unfortunate man William Lines'. After praising the victim's character, Mr Adams explained the circumstances of the case. A lawful arrest of a suspected burglar had been followed by a riot in which a uniformed Police Sergeant had been knocked to the ground and kicked and PC Lines had been stabbed while doing his duty.

The first witness was John Jenkins of the Birmingham Borough Surveyor's office who produced plans of the murder area. Mary Smith, the housekeeper at the *Bull's Head*, testified to having seen the prisoner in the pub on the night of the murder. Corkery had shouted: 'They have taken Billy,' referring to the arrest of William Downes for burglary, and had then ran out into the street.

The next witness, George Cunnington, landlord of the *Bull's Head*, explained how he had summoned the police to arrest Downes. At Cunnington's request the police cleared the pub before arresting Downes. The witness had seen Corkery in the pub, heard him cry out: 'They have taken Billy!' and had seen him run out of the pub.

Sarah Ann Hyde gave evidence about the burglary at the *Bull's Head* on Saturday 6 March. PCs Fletcher and Goodman then told the court how they had arrested Downes, to be followed by a stone-throwing mob and how they had asked PC Lines and Sergeant Fletcher to help hold it back.

James Moore, Walter Vernon, Mary Ann Conway and Ann Whalen repeated their inquest evidence to having seen the prisoner stab PC Lines. It emerged that Ann Whalen's brother, Thomas Whalen, was also accused of rioting and the defence suggested that she was lying about Corkery to protect her brother.

Two Navigation Street women, Emma Smith and Elizabeth Chatwin, also testified to having seen the stabbing.

The twelfth witness was Sergeant Fletcher. He corroborated the evidence of the other police witnesses and admitted to the defence that Thomas Whalen, Ann Whalen's brother, who was himself awaiting trial for rioting, was 'very active in the disturbances'.

The next witness, John Cruise, had seen Corkery on the Sunday morning after the murder and two days before his arrest. The prisoner was bruised on his forehead and said: 'I got knocked down with the copper's staff,' but then boasted to having retaliated by having 'chived' (stabbed) the 'copper'. The prisoner had been in hospital on 7 March the night after the murder having his bruise treated, and had tricked the hospital into putting on his card that he had been there the night before. This trick had given Corkery the false alibi he had used at the inquest which he had hoped would 'make it lighter for me'.

Margaret Morgan of Tennant Street said that on Wednesday 10 March 1875 the defendant had confessed to her that he had done the murder. However, he hoped that Aaron Rogers and Thomas Whalen, who had been in the riot, would be blamed. Later that day, Corkery had been arrested by Constable Beards who was the next witness and who described the accused's arrest.

Mr Davis, an Oldbury surgeon, testified that he had been on duty at Birmingham General Hospital on the night of the murder and had given a man a ticket. He could not definitely identify the prisoner as the person he had given a ticket to but said that the date of 6 March on the ticket was probably wrong.

Detective Seal of the Birmingham Police gave evidence that he had interrogated Corkery who had pointed out that Lines had not identified him and had named three other men instead. The victim's deposition was then read to the court in which he named Creswell, Whalen and Rogers and said that a fourth man was near him when he was stabbed.

The seventeenth and last prosecution witness, Surgeon Hamilton, of Birmingham's Queen's Hospital, described how despite medical efforts the victim had died seventeen days after being stabbed.

The Honourable E C Leigh spoke for the defence. He deplored the crime but pointed out that Ann Whalen was a sister of a major suspect in the case and that others among the prosecution witnesses were her acquaintances. He then tried to argue that in any case even if the prisoner had stabbed Lines there had been provocation since Lines had hit him with his truncheon. The judge ruled this claim out of order and Leigh summed up by saying the prisoner was being blamed for the crime of others.

The judge summed up. If anyone killed a police officer in the course of his legal duty, knowing that he was on duty, that was murder. PC Lines was in uniform so the only questions were: did the prisoner stab the victim? and had the victim been acting in accordance with his lawful authority?

It took just fifteen minutes for the jury to convict the accused of murder. The prisoner was asked if there was any reason why he should not be sentenced and he claimed to be innocent, arguing that the victim had not recognised him as his murderer and that he, of all people, ought to have known.

The judge sentenced Corkery to death. Seven other prisoners allegedly involved in the riot were tried the next day, Saturday 10 July 1875. John Cresswell, Thomas Whalen, seventeen-year-old Charles 'Barber' Mee (although he was a metal roller, his father was a barber), and eighteen-year-old tube drawer Thomas Leonard were tried and convicted for having assaulted the police with 'intent to resist and prevent the lawful apprehension and detention of William Downes, charged with burglary'. Creswell, Whalen and Leonard had criminal records for theft and Whalen also had convictions for assault, including assaulting a policeman in May 1874. In addition, it emerged that when Whalen had been arrested two days after the murder a knife had been found on him similar to the probable murder weapon. He had had time to clean it and such knives were common but the prosecution argued that this showed that he was a thug. Charles Mee had no criminal record but evidence clearly showed his heavy involvement in the riot. All four men were sentenced to life imprisonment with hard labour.

A fifth man, Thomas Kelly, a seventeen-year-old filer, was convicted of assaulting policemen in the course of their duty. He had a criminal record for theft and assault and was sentenced to five years hard labour. Two other men, Aaron Rogers, who had allegedly called PC Lines a 'pig', and eighteen-year-old brass founder Samuel McNally were acquitted.

There had been considerable witness intimidation. Several of the trial witnesses had to have police protection. One intimidator, John Hamilton, a twenty-eight-year-old Wharf Street lamp-maker, who had threatened and assaulted the prosecution witness Margaret Morgan, had been arrested, and on Thursday 1 April 1875 he had been sentenced to two months in gaol unless he could find sureties of £5, about £1,000 in modern money. His wife Margaret Hamilton was conditionally discharged for having threatened Ann Whalen.

Some of the witnesses who had axes to grind, particularly Ann Whalen, whose brother was on trial for rioting, might also have themselves been involved in such intimidation. However, the authorities might have been reluctant to charge them lest it weaken their case against Corkery. A number of alleged rioters had been released without trial and although some may have been innocent in other cases intimidation may have succeeded.

The two burglars, William Downes and Thomas Carey, were tried on Monday 12 July 1875. Carey had a long criminal record for thieving and was sentenced to fifteen years hard labour. Downes had convictions for drunkenness, vandalism and assault and was sentenced to five years hard labour. The judge admitted, in response to the defence, that Downes had quietly accepted arrest, but said that this was not a mitigating factor, though resisting it would have aggravated his offence.

Jeremiah Corkery initially seemed convinced that he would be pardoned. Petitions were got up for him but they were poorly supported and the Home Secretary rejected them. The prisoner fainted on learning that he would be hanged. He initially continued to maintain his innocence but eventually confessed to murder under the moral pressure of the prison authorities. Despite the best efforts of a Roman Catholic priest, Father Kelly, Corkery was terrified of death. He ate poorly, was unable to sleep on the night before he was due to be executed and on his last morning he could not eat breakfast.

Jeremiah Corkery was hanged inside Warwick Gaol by Mr Marwood on the morning of Wednesday 27 July 1875. The prisoner had to be dragged to the gallows and tried to stop the rope being placed around his neck by holding his chin against his chest. The hanging was witnessed by the Under Sheriff, Mr Heath, the prisoner governor, the prison surgeon, by Father Kelly and by two warders.

Was Jeremiah Corkery guilty? He was a thug with a long criminal record who had certainly taken part in a riot at the arrest of an alleged burglar who had himself wisely gone quietly. However, the witnesses' evidence against him was somewhat too coherent, suggesting that whether or not Corkery was guilty either the police and/or other interested parties had doctored it. Anyone who has seen a riot will know that it is rare for any two witnesses to give the same account of events.

There is another likely candidate for the killer. Thomas Whalen had been found in possession of a knife which was quite possibly the murder weapon but he had not been arrested until two days after the murder when he would have had ample time to clean it.

St Chad's, Birmingham's Roman Catholic Cathedral (completed in 1856),
where Jeremiah Cockery, an Irish Catholic, would have worshipped.
The author

No wonder his sister was willing to risk the wrath of the local
community by testifying against Corkery! There are also other
possible candidates for the murderer. One final point, though, is
that whoever had been charged and hanged for the murder there
would have been subsequent historians, such as myself, to point
to other possible candidates.

The *Bull's Head* closed as a pub shortly after this murder and
probably as a result. A few years later Fordrough Street itself was
demolished and Navigation Street was redeveloped, the area
ceasing to be rough and becoming part of Birmingham's central
business and shopping district. Very few buildings remain in
central Birmingham that were there in 1875, even the Public
Office that had been built in 1806 and where the inquest was held
having long since been demolished. There are still areas of
Birmingham where the police make arrests at great peril and where
witness intimidation is a major problem, as a recent notorious
double murder and other cases have shown.

Witton Cemetery remains an important cemetery. Gamgee House, the headquarters of the Birmingham Hospital Saturday Fund, a medical insurance firm, is named after Sampson 'Sam' Gamgee, the surgeon who operated on the dying PC Lines. J R R Tolkien, who lived for much of his early life in Birmingham, named one of the heroes of the *Lord of the Rings*, Sam Gamgee, after him.

CHAPTER 16

The Witch-Finder

Long Compton, 1875

Long Compton is a large south Warwickshire village near the Oxfordshire border. In 1875, the parish had a population of more than 700. The area has been continuously farmed for more than four millennium, since the Neolithic or New Stone Age when agriculture first came into Britain. In contrast, the Birmingham area was thick forest until Saxon times.

Long Compton parish houses the King's Stone, an eight foot high standing stone which is an outlier of the Rollright Stones, a Neolithic stone circle just over the Oxfordshire border. Despite Celtic, Anglo-Saxon, Viking and Norman invasions many of the 1875 Long Compton villagers were probably descendants of

The Neolithic King's Stone, Long Compton. The author

The Rollright Stones, Long Compton. The author

the people who built this stone circle and belief in the supernatural, particularly witchcraft, was widespread.

In 1875, two Long Compton villagers were seventy-nine-year-old Ann Tennant and her eighty-year-old farm labourer husband, John. Their daughter Elizabeth Hughes, the wife of a farm labourer, Thomas Hughes, also lived in the village. A forty-five-year-old farm labourer, James Haywood, became obsessed with the belief that Ann Tennant, Elizabeth Hughes and other village women were witches and were persecuting him.

At about half past seven on Wednesday 15 September 1875, Ann Tennant left her cottage to buy a loaf of bread from the grocery store kept by local farmer James Taylor. As she returned, James Haywood came past together with John Henry Evans, a fifteen-year-old farm labourer. James Haywood attacked Ann Tennant with a pitchfork which he had been earlier using at work in a field of beans. He stabbed her in the head and then in the legs. She fell over and Haywood was about to attack her again when James Taylor, who was nearby, seized him.

Elizabeth Hughes had heard her mother's screams and came to help. Ann Tennant was taken back to her daughter's house, which was closer than her own home, and her assailant was handed over to the village policeman, John Simpson, at eight that evening, half an hour after the attack.

A Chipping Norton, Oxfordshire, surgeon, George Wright Hutchinson, arrived at eleven that evening but despite his efforts the victim died soon afterwards from blood loss and shock. The next day, Thursday 16 September 1875, the killer was handed over to Superintendent James Thompson of the Shipston-on-Stour police.

An inquest was held at the *Red Lion* in Long Compton on Friday 17 September 1875. John Tennant, John Henry Evans, James Taylor, Elizabeth Hughes, PC Simpson, Superintendent Thompson and Surgeon Hutchinson gave evidence. The coroner ruled that the issue of the prisoner's sanity should be left to the assizes, and the inquest ruled that the victim had been murdered by Haywood. As the prisoner was taken from Long Compton to Warwick Gaol many angry villagers booed at him.

The 1875 Warwickshire Winter Assizes opened on Monday 13 December 1875. The judge, Mr Baron George Bramwell, in his opening speech to the grand jury, devoted much time to the Haywood case saying:

> *There was another most incredible case. It was a charge against James Haywood of killing a poor woman seventy nine years of age. There was no doubt he killed her by stabbing her with a pitchfork several times. The reason that this wretched creature did the act was that he had got it into his head that she was a witch, because he (the judge)supposed that she was labouring under the double misfortune of being old and poor and that it was a sort of religious duty on his part to put an end to her life. He need not tell them that .... there could be no such duty. When the law forbade it if a man however bona fide he might act in the execution of such a deed – if he killed a person he was guilty of murder.*

The grand jury returned a true bill against Haywood and he was tried before an ordinary jury on Wednesday 15 December 1875. The judge was Mr Baron Bramwell, the prosecution counsel were Mr Dugdale and Mr Chamberlayne, and the defence counsel was Mr Buszard.

The prosecution case was opened by Mr Dugdale who outlined the facts. John Tennant, the victim's husband, was the first witness explaining that on the murder day the victim had been at her daughter's house. She had come home to find that there was no bread in the house. She went out to get some telling her

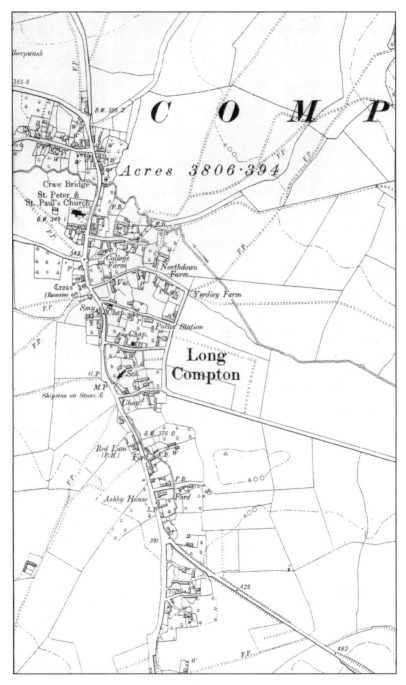

Long Compton in c.1906, from the 6 inch to 1 mile OS map. Ordnance Survey

Judge Baron Bramwell, who tried James Haywood. Birmingham Library

husband to 'attend to the fire in the meantime'.

John Tennant said that the prisoner and the prisoner's parents had been next door neighbours of the Tennants for thirty years and were firm witchcraft believers. The parents would lock their cottage door ,even when they went out, to get coal from their coalhouse. They would say things like: 'They are at that boy again. It is those witches; they will not let that boy alone.'

John Tennant further said that the prisoner's 'conduct was not much otherwise than that of a madman'. He was 'always talking about witches' and his behaviour had been aggravated by hurting his head falling out of a tree. The prisoner was a heavy drinker and was regarded as 'soft' by the local farmers and other villagers and as a result was often jobless.

The second witness was fifteen-year-old John Henry Evans. On the murder evening he had been walking home with Haywood who had been carrying a two pronged pitchfork, and a bottle and basket. Haywood said that there were fifteen witches in the village and he would kill them all. When the accused saw the victim he put down his bottle and basket and attacked her with the pitch-fork.

James Taylor was the next witness. He had been in his orchard at the time of the attack, had heard the victim crying: 'Oh dear' three times and ran to help her. He seized her assailant who said that there were 'fifteen or sixteen . . . witches in the parish; he had killed one and he would kill the rest'.

The witness had known the prisoner since his boyhood. He was a good worker, despite the victim's husband's somewhat biased evidence, but he was somewhat 'strange at times' and 'harboured ideas about evil spirits and witches'. The prisoner had earlier on the day of the murder told the witness that witches had haunted him for three hours preventing him from working.

Apart from the subject of witches, the prisoner was normally sane except when he was 'in beer'. The witness explained that the prisoner had said that his master had given him a gallon of ale on the day of the murder. It was standard practise for harvest workers to be given beer but not for them to drink such an amount too quickly. Some days before the attack the accused had consulted a Coughton, Warwickshire, 'water doctor' or spiritualist, Mr Manning.

Elizabeth Hughes, the victim's daughter, was the next witness. On seeing her in court the prisoner exclaimed, 'There is another witch there.' She described how she had heard her mother scream and had come to help her. The prisoner had said 'I've done it, I've done it, I meant to do it; and there are several more I mean to serve the same.' The witness described how the accused had believed that witches were tormenting him and how he frequently talked about them but was ignored by the villagers who considered him a 'wild man.' The prisoner had even once warned the witness to 'keep away from the aged women as they would make me as bad as themselves.'

The fifth witness was PC Simpson who had arrested Haywood after the attack. When he had warned his prisoner that his victim would probably die he had replied, 'No odds about it; I hope she is dead. There is a lot more I will serve the same.' The prisoner had claimed that witches had stopped him from working for three hours. PC Simpson said that that this was probably due to drunkenness. He said that the prisoner had been normally 'a quiet peaceable man' and that many Long Compton people believed in witchcraft. Both the prisoner's parents had been nonconformists.

Superintendent Thompson then testified. On being told that the victim was dead the prisoner had said: 'Dead, dead; I did not kill her outright.' The prisoner was cautioned and said nothing more until the next day, 16 September 1875, when he described having seen witches in a water bottle saying that only people who were bewitched could see them.

The seventh and last prosecution witness was Surgeon Hutchinson who described the victim's wounds. There was a punctured pitchfork wound on her left temple, two such wounds on her right leg below the knee, and three on the left leg. Her head was badly bruised where she had fallen heavily. The leg wounds had penetrated varicose veins and death had been caused by bleeding and shock. In cross examination Surgeon Hutchinson said that the prisoner was one of his patients and had seemed rational. Hutchinson confirmed that there was a 'wise man' or 'water doctor', Mr Manning, living 'near Banbury', a curious description of Coughton.

The defence set about proving Haywood's insanity. The first defence witness, Mr J M Anderson, the Governor of Warwick Gaol, described the prisoner as 'pretty shrewd upon some matters; but his general bearing was that of an eccentric weak minded man'.

Haywood had quoted bible passages to justify his crime, including Leviticus and the prophet Micah from the Old Testament, and the Acts of the Apostles from the New Testament. He had requested a jug and a small phial and the next morning had produced the phial which was full of his own urine. Holding the phial up to the light, the prisoner claimed that a small air bubble was proof that he was 'possessed'. The prisoner blamed his victim for 'possessing' him and others and stopping him from working, having 'looked' at him (given him the 'evil eye').

Mr Anderson said that the defendant seemed sane on every subject except witchcraft: 'His delusion on the subject of witches was very strong indeed.'

The next defence witness was Dr Parsey, the Medical Superintendent at Hatton Lunatic Asylum, who had examined Haywood on the 21 and 24 September 1875. The prisoner had been 'of feeble mind, of eager childish manner, and with a loud discordant tone of voice'. Although the accused had been aware that he was in trouble, and was anxious about his position, he failed to realise the gravity of his offence.

The prisoner had claimed that he had merely intended to draw his victim's blood to break her power over him. Although he had not meant to kill her, he did not regret her death quoting the biblical book of Leviticus. He had enumerated thirteen other alleged Long Compton witches who he blamed for all his ailments and stopping him working. Sometime before the attack the prisoner had visited a Coughton 'cunning man', Mr Manning, who had taught the prisoner how to use water to detect witches.

The prisoner had a large scar on his head, presumably caused by him having fallen out of a tree. He was hard of hearing and had a speech impediment. Surgeon Parsey did not believe that the accused would ever get better and said that if he were found insane he would have to spend the rest of his life in an asylum.

In cross-examination Dr Parsey said that in South Warwickshire belief in witchcraft and possession were common. The difference between ordinary believers in witches and the accused was that ordinary sane people merely believed that witches existed, while the accused believed that they were constantly tormenting him. Many of the Hatton Asylum patients believed that they were bewitched and often people would say that their patient relatives were bewitched rather than insane.

The third and last defence witness was J R Nunn, the Warwick County Gaol surgeon. He said that the prisoner had 'entertained a strong belief in witches' and had believed that he was possessed. In cross-examination, Surgeon Nunn said that the accused had acted impulsively and would have acted the same no matter who was nearby. Dr Parsey said that lunatics often acted impulsively and completely out of character.

Mr Buszard then made a speech defending Haywood, arguing that the prisoner was completely deluded and should be acquitted

Long Compton's medieval church and Tudor lynchgate. The author

as insane. The judge then summed up, saying that 'during the twenty years he had sat on the bench he never remembered such a melancholy and terrible case . . . A poor helpless old creature . . . had been killed by the accused, whilst labouring under the influence of a superstition and ignorance discreditable to a set of savages, let alone to a civilized country like England'. The judge 'doubted very much whether there was in this case much of the impulse spoken to by the medical gentlemen'. From the way in which the prisoner had on the way home spoken of the witches and of his intention to kill them, he thought it was much more a case of intention.

Despite the judge's comments, the jury took only a few minutes to acquit Haywood as insane. The judge, in disgust, said that he had clearly laid down the law to the jury and could not help their verdict, and sentenced the prisoner to be detained at Her Majesty's Pleasure. The judge was himself sixty-seven and was only twelve years younger than the victim and much older than most of the jury.

Much remains in Long Compton that was there in 1875 including its medieval church and its two-storey Elizabethan lychgate, and the *Red Lion*, where the inquest was held. Nearby, the Rollright Stones attract visitors. In 1971, aged eleven, I visited them with my mother, an ATS veteran, who was stationed nearby during the Second World War. There were then local villagers who knew people who were involved in the case and some such people may well still be alive today, in 2006.

In 1875 the witchcraft mania of the seventeenth century was only two long lifetimes away and much of Long Compton was still living in the past despite the railways, the electric telegraph and great scientific advances. After all, even in our age of space travel and genetic engineering the furore over J K Rowling's Harry Potter books shows that many people still believe in the supernatural.

CHAPTER 17

The Fortune-Teller

Birmingham, 1882 & 1883

I n 1882, John Hartwell was twenty-eight. A fortune-teller, he lived in High Street, West Bromwich but operated from 97 Bracebridge Street, Birmingham. He worked through newspaper adverts and the post using various pseudonyms including 'Methratton the Great Seer of England', 'Anna Ross the Seeress of New York', 'The Sybil', and the 'philosopher, astrologer, grandmaster of the mysteries, enchanter, sorcerer and dealer in magic and spells.'

For Hartwell's prophecies, people had to send at least two and sixpence (c.£25 today) though they were encouraged to send larger sums. Prophecies would be accompanied by small square, brown paper 'charms' and, to avoid the laws against fortune-telling, cheap German prints so he could claim that he was selling prints rather than prophecies.

Despite his precautions, on 17 May 1882, Hartwell appeared at the Birmingham Police Court, the magistrates being Mr Kynnersley the stipendiary and Mr Lord. Detective Inspector Helden of the Birmingham police testified that he could prove three cases of charging for fortune-telling against the prisoner but only one was presented. Mrs Mary Ann Wall, of 97 Bracebridge Street, gave evidence that the prisoner had first lodged with her and then used her house as a mail drop. The Walls had often laughed at Hartwell's claims but had readily taken his money.

The third and main witness was Miss Ellis Potter, of Huddersfield, Yorkshire, to whom the prisoner had been recommended by a friend. She had sent two and six and received this letter:

April. Dear Madam – I have given my best attentions to the particulars of your destiny, and find that the sun, who today shone in the glorious firmament, is your planetary genius. Imitate you his steady career, for your nativity foretells many great adventures and exploits – indeed you will be most fortunate in the world, to a degree that may astonish your present contemporaries – but ill fortune or a few cares in early life will come upon you. Wednesday will be your most noted day for good fortune, Saturday for evil; and the seventeenth day of the month will prove a day of great note in your horoscope of fate. Look well to your intentions – the course of your love will resemble that of a shallow brook which dashing over numerous impediments, is yet thwarted by a mountain. But a prudent husband is yours after all harm is past. There appears many an emblem ominous enough in some joyous event, as it relates to your family. Even now are the celestial omens more successful and flattering than of late; and you will have most friends. Go westward if for gain, eastward if for honour or fame and the whole bias of your fate turns on a certain journey at a future period of your life. There is a change approaching in your horoscope of fate; take due advantage of it. You would succeed in skilful trades or in dealing with the rich and attending to the wishes of the wealthy, also in travelling, voyaging, and visiting distant lands and by foreigners – I am etc. RAOB. Cabinet print enclosed for the 2s 6d.

Miss Potter had a good memory and recognised the letter as an exact copy of one she had paid sixpence (c.£5 today) for to an allegedly different fortune-teller in 1875. Realising they were from the same man, she sent this letter:

Huddersfield, April 24, 1882. Dear Sir, Yours to hand last night. I find it an exact copy of the one enclosed which you sent me in the year 1875. Now in common fairness to me, I am going to ask a few questions as I feel sure things are a little different now to what they were then, and if you answer them with all fairness I shall be quite satisfied with the rest. I don't think for one moment that I am asking more than is my due and you cannot help seeing the fairness of it. Now in the first place you say there is a change approaching. Is the change still approaching? If so, am I going to take another situation or is it at all connected with the 'joyous events' in family? Will you also explain a little more clearly about my 'looking well to my intentions' also about 'the course of my love resembling a shallow brook' and the 'whole bias of my fate turning on a certain journey?'. Is that journey still far off or is it connected with the approaching change; and my being fortunate will it be from parents, or husband or both. Please do not feel at all anxious about my finding you out under another name for believe me your secret is quite safe. I have also taken the precautions to cut the name out also the name of the town before I send it. I am returning the cabinet print but you can again send it to me. Awaiting your answer, yours etc, (signed) E. POTTER.

Hartwell ignored this letter and Miss Potter had contacted the police and risked ridicule by travelling to Birmingham and testifying. The prisoner claimed that he had only charged for the print rather than for his prophecies, which had been made in good faith. Amid much laughter he was sentenced to four months in gaol.

On leaving prison, Hartwell resumed fortune-telling, working from both Bracebridge Street and the nearby Miller Street. On 15 January 1883, he was arrested again and on Tuesday 30 January 1883, he was tried at Birmingham Police Court, again by Mr Kynnersley.

The first witness was a young lady, Miss Elizabeth Grant, of Belgrave, Leicester. Friends had recommended Hartwell to her and she had seen his adverts in the press for instance: 'The great prophet will reveal your future seven years, 7d; marriage and other particulars 2s 6d; how to cause lover's visits 2s 6d; wonderful supernatural records 1s 6d and five 5s – Methratton, 137, Miller Street, Birmingham' and 'The future seven years, seven stamps; love talisman sixteen stamps; send age. Reply RAOB.'

In reply to her letter, Miss Grant was advised to delay marriage because at that time everything would go wrong but if she postponed it she would be able to marry a rich husband. The witness had burnt the letter but identified letters found by the police as being in the same handwriting.

The second witness, Mrs Bessie Foxley of 139 Miller Street, Birmingham, testified that the prisoner had left a box at her house, shortly before Christmas 1882. The police had seized this box. The next witness, Mrs Esther Powell of 137 Miller Street, said that the prisoner had lodged at her house for three weeks and had later used it as a mail drop, receiving three or four letters a day on average.

The fourth and last witness was Detective Sergeant Ashby of the Birmingham police. On 15 January 1883, he had arrested Hartwell at his Bracebridge Street address just after Hartwell had received four letters from the postman, three being addressed 'Methratton' and one 'Mr Methratton'. One letter contained thirty-one stamps 'for marriage and all particulars'.

The Detective Sergeant later raided Mrs Foxley's house at 139 Miller Street and found a box containing more than 300 letters from Hartwell's customers, nearly all young ladies though one was a sailor who wanted to know if he would be going to sea all his life. It also contained a copy of Hartwell's price list which ranged up to £50 for 'elixir and tree of life secrets'.

Evidence was produced as to the prisoner's previous conviction at Birmingham in 1882 and to others for fortune-telling at Daventry and London; and for selling 'indecent literature' at London for which he had served eighteen months. In his defence the prisoner claimed to be a genuine prophet and said that his terms of imprisonment had been accompanied by national disasters and that if he was sent to prison again England would be ruined.

Mr Kynnersley convicted the accused but decided that as a magistrate he lacked adequate sentencing powers, so he ruled that the prisoner should be sent to hard labour and that a decision as to his sentence should be made at the Quarter Sessions.

On Wednesday 28 March 1883, Hartwell appeared at the Quarter Sessions. The judge was the Recorder of Birmingham, John Stratford Dugdale QC. Elizabeth Grant, Mrs Foxley, Mrs Powell, and Detective Sergeant Ashby gave evidence again.

The Recorder said that the prisoner had twice been confined in lunatic asylums in Northamptonshire and at Macclesfield. Captain Tinklar the Governor of Birmingham Gaol said that he had no medical evidence that the prisoner was insane. Having settled this point the Recorder told the Clerk of the Court to read one of the accused's letters to 'one of those stupid people' to warn the public. It read:

Dear Madam I have given my best attentions to the particulars of your destiny and find that by mysterious omens the sign Libra . . . bears rule over your fate which tells of the hazards of chance; a rise beyond your expectations, a prosperous name and the gifts of wealth; and by other means you will be fortunate in this world; you will have fair abodes, rich habitations and enjoy the luxuries of fortune. The star governing wedlock in your horoscope tells of a great adventure in love and a surprise therein. You have the sign of a prosperous marriage with one tall and good looking and a favourite with both sexes. Bold and adventurous even as Mars who rules the omens is ever found to be so will be your family, or the real or adopted [sic], and fortunate in the main. Your fate is at present unsettled and prone to change. Choose mostly the westward rivers and the sea and places where navigable rivers or large bodies of water are. This refers both to travelling or residence. You will be an adept and prosper in almost everything you would undertake but had best deal (that is if you go into business for yourself) in substances produced from the earth. The signs speak of two friends which will cause you much happiness. A solar fair person tall, yellow or brown hair and in a good position in society will ere long become your bosom friend. I am yours truly METHRATTON.

Love charm 16d. This is marriage and other particulars 2s 6d, stamps; three questions same price. Thursday is the chief day of your life both in adversity and prosperity. Search well in your past life and you will already find it so. Do nothing afresh in the month of January nor yet in the wane or decrease of the moon.

In his defence, Hartwell claimed to have acted legally having sold 'sacred art (the German prints) and supplied his prophecies gratis. Miracles had happened to him for instance once a key had magically left his pocket and another time a missing key had miraculously turned up. Since his childhood he had seen visions and heard voices. He was wealthy, owned property in London and Daventry, and came from a good family, being a grandson of Lord Lovat.

Concerning the legality of his fortune-telling, the prisoner claimed to have been acting on the advice of a *Daily Telegraph* article some years before, of a solicitor, and of a barrister to whom he had paid £5. Many upper and middle class people consulted him including clergy and a woman missionary in India. He claimed to have been waging 'the holy and mysterious millennial war' since 1865, when he was eleven, and to have predicted the 1 September 1876 storm three months before.

After hearing this defence, the Recorder sentenced Hartwell to nine months in gaol, saying that the prisoner had apparently imagined that he was acting legally. Despite the prisoner's earlier forecasts of supernatural doom, Mr Dugdale lived until 1920 when he died aged eighty-five.

The prisoner had fooled gullible people out of their often hard-earned money. On the other hand, the prosecutions had absorbed police time which could have been spent tracking down burglars. As my paternal grandfather, who was born in 1882 often said: 'A fool and his money are soon parted.'

Few buildings remain in central Birmingham that were there in 1882. However, Bracebridge Street and Miller Street are on the edge between Birmingham and Aston where many buildings survive that were there in 1882, including the seventeenth century Aston Hall and the medieval parish church.

CHAPTER 18

The Poisoner

Leamington Spa, 1889

I n 1800, Leamington Spa was called Leamington Priors. In 1811, the parish had 543 inhabitants, some of them in the surrounding rural area, and in 1812 the village contained sixty houses. For the next two generations it boomed as a spa town where the well-off came to take the waters. In 1814, the Pump Rooms opened and by 1831 the spa had 6,269 residents, having grown more than eleven times in two decades. In 1838, Queen Victoria let Leamington call itself Royal Leamington Spa and by 1841 the population had increased to 12,600. The growth rate then slowed but remained respectable and, by 1881, Leamington, having been incorporated as a town in 1875, had

The Pump Rooms, Leamington Spa. The author

25,141 people having grown more than forty times in one lifetime.

The 1880s saw economic depression and a decline in Leamington's base as a spa as its former wealthy customers increasingly took foreign holidays. Population growth temporarily stagnated, poverty increased and jobs were in short supply.

In February 1889, three well off Leamington Spa residents were Dr William Robert Horniblow, an Edinburgh University-trained doctor who lived and worked at 76 Clarendon Street, his wife Elizabeth who was genteelly described in the press as a lady of 'mature years', and their fourteen-year-old son, William Henry Horniblow. They employed Sarah Kibbler as an occasional char-woman. The press alternatively described her as 'an elderly woman' and 'a woman of middle age', and she lived with her husband and daughter at 23 St George's Road. The Horniblows kept a pet rat in a cage over the scullery fireplace, calling it 'Tibbins'. It was mainly looked after by Elizabeth who would feed it milk, potatoes, biscuits, cake and sugar and sometimes take it to bed with her and kiss and cuddle it.

On 14 February 1889, Elizabeth had a stroke which left her left

Clarenden Street, Leamington. The author

The Clarendon Street house where the victim lived. The author

side paralysed. On 16 February, Sarah Kibbler took up full-time employment as a maid of all work and nurse for the Horniblows. Her duties included looking after the pet rat which she detested. Sarah came to hope that Elizabeth's death would let her keep her full time job. Elizabeth started to recover and said: 'I am so glad I did not die; I do not know what would become of the doctor and my little boy.' Sarah replied: 'Oh I think he would have done very well; I could have come and taken care of the house and my old man (her husband) could have cleaned the knives and boots and taken care of the garden.'

On 7 March 1889, Sarah made a cup of tea for Elizabeth. Elizabeth drank about half but found it very nasty, tasting of 'copper and Lucifer matches.' On being challenged, Sarah said that she had put sugar in it by mistake but the victim realised this was a lie. About five minutes later Elizabeth felt great internal pain and was violently sick several times, vomiting blood. She recovered after her husband later gave her castor oil as a purgative.

On 14 March 1889, Sarah Kibbler told Joseph Bellamy, a Leamington milkman, that Elizabeth Horniblow was 'much worse' and was dying. Sarah said that Elizabeth had heard a man's footsteps on the landing when no one was there. Dr Horniblow allegedly said that this was a death omen, so Bellamy was very surprised to see Elizabeth Horniblow out on the street on 15 March.

The Horniblows' pet rat died on 18 March having been ill for several days. It was 'cremated' in the kitchen fire. The family, especially Elizabeth, were distressed but Sarah Kibbler was openly pleased.

On 23 March, Elizabeth Horniblow felt ill. She mixed herself a glass of hot water and brandy in the kitchen. She then left the kitchen and Sarah Kibbler brought her the brandy and water. It tasted like the poisoned tea and the intended victim said: 'Oh Mrs Kibbler, how disagreeable this brandy is; it is exactly like the tea.' According to Elizabeth, Sarah Kibbler then 'whipped up the end of the tablecloth and sent the liquor in the cup over my dress'.

By this time the Horniblows were very suspicious of their servant and on 6 April 1889 she was sacked but they could not yet prove anything. On Easter Thursday, 18 April, Dr Horniblow took down the dead rat's cage to get rid of it. He found some suspicious looking powder on its floor. He analysed some of it and found it was mercuric chloride or what he called 'corrosive sublimate', a very strong poison whose symptoms would account for the taste of the poisoned cup of tea and glass of brandy and water, and for the pet rat's death. In tiny doses, mercuric chloride was used to treat syphilis and Dr Horniblow checked his surgery bottle to find a great deal missing.

The next day, Good Friday, Dr and Mrs Horniblow's son searched the family bins, finding two pieces of the broken cup which had been smashed when the suspect snatched up the tablecloth. On one of the pieces, to which the handle was still attached, mercuric chloride traces were found.

On Sunday 27 April 1889, there occurred a scene that could have come from one of Conan Doyle's Sherlock Holmes tales, the first of which had been published two years earlier. Dr Horniblow invited Sarah Kibbler to his house and challenged her about his discoveries. He intended to trick her into merely confessing to poisoning the rat thus giving him the basis for a charge of trying to poison his wife that could be presented to the police. The suspect 'went into a state of the greatest terror and asked to be forgiven' both by Dr Horniblow and by Elizabeth who the good doctor forced her to confront as, though partially recovered, she lay on her sickbed. Dr Horniblow suggested that if the Kibblers left Leamington he would let matters drop but Sarah's husband refused.

After this scene, Dr Horniblow finally asked the Leamington
Spa police to prosecute Sarah Kibbler for attempted murder. The
police, who then as now intensely disliked amateur detectives,
refused and the doctor consulted his lawyer, taking out a private
prosecution.

On Wednesday 1 May 1889, the case was heard before four
Leamington Spa magistrates: Alderman Flavel (the Mayor of
Leamington), Aldermen Edelmann and Wackrill and Councillor
Dr Thursfield. Mr Crowther Davies conducted the prosecution
and Mr Sanderson the defence. The three Horniblows testified for
the prosecution.

Dr Horniblow's case was not helped by a prolonged argument
over whether he should take the usual oath or rather affirm an
option which had been created in 1888, a year before, so that
agnostics and atheists could have full civil rights without denying
their principles. Dr Horniblow said that he did not consider the
bible a divine book but the magistrates pointed out that he had
earlier sworn on the bible to the information on which the warrant
arresting Sarah Kibbler had been issued. Eventually, Dr
Horniblow took the normal oath on a bible but this argument did

St George's Road where the prisoner lived. The author

not help him and the magistrates eventually refused to commit the accused.

Dr Horniblow took matters further. First, he contacted Dr Alfred Bostock Hill, the Warwickshire Public Analyst, who analysed material taken from the rat's cage and the broken cup. He found traces of mercuric chloride and found that the amount of material on the cup could easily have proved fatal, even though it must have been a fraction of the actual dose. Only the victim's prompt vomiting had saved her life. Joseph Bellamy also reported his strange conversation with the suspect, for the Leamington Spa press had heavily publicised the magistrates' court proceedings

The Horniblows contacted the Director of Public Prosecutions (the DPP), Sir Augustus Stephenson with this evidence. This post had been created by the 1879 Prosecution of Offenders Act. The DPP decided that there was a valid case against Sarah Kibbler and his staff presented a charge to the 1889 Warwick Summer Assizes. On Wednesday 31 July 1889, the grand jury found a true bill against the accused but the judge, Sir Henry Hawkins, ruled that the actual trial should be left to the Winter Assizes to give both prosecution and defence time to prepare their cases. The accused was allowed bail.

Sarah Kibbler was tried at the Warwick Winter Assizes on Monday 16 December 1889. The judge was Mr Justice Wills, the prosecution was conducted by Mr Fitzgerald, who was instructed by Mr Crowther Davies, and the defence counsel was Hugo Young, who was instructed by Mr Sanderson.

Mr Fitzgerald presented the prosecution case and the three Horniblows, Joseph Bellamy and Dr Bostock Hill then testified. There was again discussion as to whether Dr Horniblow should take an oath or affirm. The doctor said that he agreed with the views of Thomas Arnold's son, Matthew Arnold, the school inspector, poet, writer and religious thinker on this matter who, although a strong Anglican, denied that the bible was a divine book. The judge refused to let the court be side-tracked into such a discussion and let the witness decide himself as to if he should take an oath or affirm. The witness took the normal oath on the bible, explaining that he always told the truth anyway.

In cross-examination the defence challenged as to why the victim and her family had taken so long to act. It was explained that the victim had a bad memory and had not told her husband of all her symptoms at first. Dr Horniblow said that he had not challenged the prisoner about them initially, saying that he was not the first doctor to have omitted to discuss his wife's illness with the family charwoman. The defence also produced evidence that

Jephson Gardens. The author

the local council had emptied the Horniblows's bins before the discovery of the broken cup pieces but it was explained that the family had several bins.

Mr Young spoke for the defence. He admitted that the prisoner had poisoned the rat and suggested that the upset and resentful Horniblows had tried to frame her for poisoning Elizabeth. He argued that the poisoned tea cup had been accidentally contaminated by the rat having got poison on it from its cage, while being played with by the victim who then got some of it into her tea. He suggested that as for the brandy glass the accused had put the poison in it to deal with rats and that the victim had not seen this when she put brandy and water in it. The incident with the tablecloth could have been an accident.

The judge summed up. He was hostile to the prisoner and was surprised that the Leamington magistrates had refused to commit her. The jury took a long time over their deliberations but eventually convicted the accused of attempted murder. The judge sentenced her to fifteen years' hard labour.

The growth of Leamington Spa was much slower last century than in the nineteenth century merely doubling in size rather than growing more than forty fold. As a result, much of the town remains that would be recognised by the Horniblows, including the Victorian parish church of All Saints and the lovely Jephson Gardens. The Pump Rooms were rebuilt in 1926, though the Tuscan-style 1814 colonnade survives. Remember, though, that what we see as a historic town was in its Victorian heyday a rapidly expanding new town. Beneath its professionally genteel facade was an often raw core.

CHAPTER 19

The Abortionist

Aston, 1895 & 1896

By 1895, Aston was part of Birmingham's urban sprawl though it had is own borough council and its police force was part of the Warwickshire Constabulary rather than the Birmingham one. One resident was Mrs Sarah Ann Eden, a fifty-seven-year-old midwife, who was married with children, and who lived at 34 Leonard Road in the area where Aston merges with Handsworth. Although she had a good midwifery practice working with local doctors, Mrs Eden doubled as an abortionist despite abortion then being illegal. One client was Mabel Gordon, a twenty-four-year-old barmaid and book-keeper at the *Albion Hotel*, Leeds.

Mabel was five months pregnant and her abortion was arranged by John Hindson, aged forty-three, a commercial traveller who sold paints and varnishes. Although Hindson had a wife and children in Hull he had lady friends in at least three cities, including Isabella Pirie of 235 Union Road, Aberdeen, a shop assistant who imagined that they were engaged; Matilda Manning, aged thirty-three, a dressmaker, of 13 Victoria Road, Aston; and Mabel Gordon in Leeds.

Mabel was originally from Aberdeen. Hindson wrote to his Aberdeen girlfriend Isabella Pirie that Mabel had got pregnant and was close to child birth, and that both her family and the *Albion Hotel's* proprietors, were very strict religious people who would respectively disown and sack her if they found out. On the advice of Hindson's letters, Isabella telegrammed Mabel, asking her to return home as her mother in Aberdeen was ill. This then covered for Mabel's journey from Leeds to Aston on Wednesday 16 October 1895. She stayed with Matilda Manning and on 17 October 1895 Mrs Eden aborted her baby at Matilda's house, 13 Victoria Road Aston.

Hindson sent a letter to Miss Pirie telling her that Mabel had successfully given birth. Miss Pirie sent another telegram to the *Albion Hotel* ostensibly saying that Mabel's mother was much improved and that Mabel could return to Leeds. On Thursday 24

Part of Aston, from a map dated 1900. Birmingham Library

October 1895, Mabel returned to Leeds and on 26 October she died of peritonitis at the *Albion Hotel.*

Another client of Mrs Eden was Rebecca Simister, aged thirty-three, the wife of Thomas Simister, a boot-maker, of 170 High Street, Aston. The Simisters had six children, all but the first having been delivered by Mrs Eden. Rebecca was in poor health and her last childbirth had been very difficult.

On Wednesday 23 October 1895, Rebecca left home at ten in the morning and visited Mrs Eden who used a sharp instrument to abort her baby. Rebecca returned home at about twelve noon. Thomas Simister returned home at half-past three in the afternoon to find his wife sitting in a chair downstairs. She then went to bed, leaving her husband to mind the house.

At half past seven in the morning, on Thursday 24 October, Thomas Simister got up. Half an hour later his wife, the abortion having taken effect, gave him the foetus of what would have been their seventh child. She had wrapped it in paper and asked him to throw it away.

On Friday 25 October, Rebecca was still ill and Thomas asked her if she wanted a doctor. She refused but on Saturday morning she agreed to call Mrs Eden. Mrs Eden came and saw that her patient/victim was very ill. On her urgent recommendation Dr Fairley, of Lozells Road, was called, but he was out on business, so Dr Garvey came. Despite Mrs Eden's pleas, Rebecca told Dr Garvey what had happened. Despite medical help, Rebecca died at about half past five on Tuesday 29 October 1895. Thomas Simister said to Eden: 'You are the cause of all my trouble. You have robbed me of my wife and my children of their mother.' Mrs Eden replied: 'What I have done I have done for her good. I would not have done anything to hurt her, I loved her so.' A post-mortem confirmed that the deceased's death had been due to peritonitis caused by an abortion.

The Leeds and Aston police forces became involved. Whether this was due to two separate lines of inquiry merging or because of one inquiry unearthing other information is unclear. On Wednesday 30 October Mrs Sarah Ann Eden and Miss Matilda Manning appeared before the Aston magistrates and were remanded in custody. Mrs Eden was charged with murdering Rebecca Simister and Mabel Gordon. Matilda Manning was charged with involvement in the murder of Mabel Gordon.

An inquest into Rebecca Simister's death was opened at the *Barton Arms* in Aston on Friday 1 November 1895. The coroner was Mr Joseph Ansell. Thomas Simister, his sister Annie Simister, Dr Garvey and Detective Inspector Ravenhall of the Aston police

The *Barton Arms* where the inquest into Rebecca Simister's death was held.
The author

gave evidence. The inquest returned a verdict that Rebecca Simister had been murdered by Mrs Sarah Ann Eden. Any inquest into Mabel Gordon's death was held in Leeds therefore is beyond the scope of this book.

On Wednesday 6 November 1895, Eden and Manning appeared before the Aston magistrates. John Hindson was the principal witness against Manning explaining how he had arranged for Mabel Gordon to visit her so that Mrs Eden could abort Mabel's baby. His evidence as to Mabel's movements was corroborated by that of Ellen Elizabeth Mason, the housekeeper at the *Albion Hotel* where Mabel had worked. Matilda Manning's defence counsel Hugo Young successfully got the charge against his client reduced from murder to manslaughter and she was allowed bail.

Mrs Eden was less lucky. As well as the evidence given at the inquest Dr G P Adamson, of Birchfield Road, Handsworth, corroborated the medical evidence. Apart from repeating his earlier evidence Detective Inspector Ravenhall produced a sharp instrument of the type used to perform abortions, that had been found in a vase at Mrs Eden's 34 Leonard Street house. The prisoner was committed for trial at the next Assizes, bail being refused.

Sarah Ann Eden was tried at the Warwickshire Assizes on Tuesday 10 December 1895. The judge was Mr Justice Day, the prosecution counsel were Mr Soden and Mr Keep and the prisoner was defended by Mr Dorsett. Thomas Simister testified as to what had happened and was corroborated by his sister, Annie Simister. Drs Garvey, Adamson and Fairley gave medical evidence and Detective Inspector Ravenhall reported the prisoner's semi-confession in which she admitted to being an abortionist but denied having used sharp instruments.

The defence attempted to get the charge against Eden reduced to manslaughter, pointing out that the accused had not intended to kill the victim and had even suggested calling a doctor when things had clearly gone wrong. The judge summed up saying that all the jury had to decide was whether the accused had performed an illegal operation; and had it caused the victim's death.

The all-male jury took ten minutes to convict Mrs Eden of murder and the judge sentenced her to death, making a speech condemning abortion which he said was a practise intended 'to relieve women of the consequences of their own indulgence' and which in fact caused many deaths each year. It was decided not to try Mrs Eden on the charge of murdering Mabel Gordon.

Matilda Manning was then tried for manslaughter. Ellen Elizabeth Mason gave her evidence and then John Hindson testified. As he testified, his own involvement became increasingly clear, despite a belated warning from the judge to avoid self incrimination. There was a brief interruption to proceedings when the foreman of the jury had an epileptic fit and had to be carried from the courtroom. The judge then consulted with the prosecution and defence counsel. All charges against Matilda Manning were dropped and instead John Hindson was arrested on a murder charge!

Public attitude to Eden's condemnation was mixed. On the one hand a *Birmingham Evening Mail* editorial described her as a 'professional trafficker in infanticide' and a 'wicked old hag' but the same editorial said that 'there is something specially hideous in the idea of a woman being condemned to hang' and called her a 'wretched old woman'. Although there were cases where the editorialist thought that women might deserve hanging, this was not one.

By 15 December 1895 more than 10,000 people had signed a petition calling for Mrs Eden to be reprieved. Among the

Vanity Fair cartoon of Sir Benjamin Stone. Birmingham Library

signatories were at least half the jury. Supporters of the campaign for her reprieve included the Aston Manor Conservative MP Captain George William Grice-Hutchinson a veteran of the Zulu Wars; Sir Benjamin Stone the glass manufacturer, Conservative MP for East Birmingham and locally famous amateur photographer; and Mr James Henry Yoxall the Liberal MP for Nottingham West and General Secretary of the National Union of Teachers.

The following letter appeared in the *Birmingham Gazette* on 16 December 1895:

I herewith beg to endorse your plea for mercy in the case of the singularly unfortunate woman condemned for murder. My argument is that two blacks do not make one white. My own wife's qualified nurse was visited by a lady in her carriage and offered a £5 note to perform the operation for which Mrs Eden was condemned to death. The object was to hide a single woman's shame. In declining to accede to such a crime the nurse met with abuse and was told that she ought to want bread. This I consider to be a great temptation and suggests to my mind that many poor women could not withstand. Yours faithfully – A FATHER.

There were other similar letters.

On 18 December 1895, the newspapers reported that the Conservative Home Secretary Sir Matthew White Ridley had reprieved Mrs Eden. Her sentence was commuted to hard labour for life. Sir Matthew's great grandson, Nicholas Ridley (1929–1993), was to sit in Mrs Thatcher's cabinet.

Meanwhile, proceedings against Hindson went on. On

Sir Matthew White Ridley, the Home Secretary who pardoned Mrs Eden and John Hindson. Birmingham Library

Monday 23 December 1895, he appeared before the Aston magistrates. Isabella Pirie gave evidence as did Matilda Manning. Ellen Dale, a Handsworth barmaid, testified to having seen Mabel Gordon and Mrs Eden at Matilda Manning's house on the relevant days. Albert Smith Green, a Leeds surgeon, said that Mabel Gordon, who had been five months pregnant before her abortion, had died of peritonitis at the *Albion Hotel* on 29 October 1895. Detective Inspector Ravenhall testified to having arrested the prisoner at the Warwick Assizes on the judge's orders. The magistrates decided that the evidence against Hindson was strong and he was committed on a murder charge.

John Hindson was tried at the Warwickshire Assizes on Tuesday 10 March 1896. The judge was Mr Justice Mathew, the prosecution counsel were Mr Soden and Mr Keep and the defence counsel were Hugo Young, Mr Dorsett, and Mr Horace Rowlands.

The first witness was Isabella Pirie. The correspondence between Hindson and herself was read in court, for instance, the following passage from a letter in which Hindson asked the upright Pirie to deceive Mabel Gordon's Leeds employers:

This a thing I hardly like asking you to do dear but it is a girl in trouble and although I have nothing to do with it I am not void of sympathy. I have sisters and although they have never been in this fix I cannot help doing what I can even for a stranger in this fix.

Another passage from a letter asking Pirie to cable the *Albion Hotel* so that Mabel Gordon could return home, read:

The affair (i.e. the baby that Pirie had been fooled into thinking that Mabel Gordon was having) arrived on Friday – one of your own persuasion and I suppose a very fine specimen too.

The next witness was Matilda Manning who had known the prisoner for six years and at whose house Mabel Gordon had miscarried having been aborted by Mrs Eden. Her correspondence also revealed Hindson as a plausible rat.

The third witness, Sarah Ann Eden, was brought from her prison cell. She was still equivocal about her role as an abortionist but confirmed to having met Matilda Manning and Mabel Gordon together.

Mr William Walker, the assistant clerk to the Aston justices, testified as to how Hindson had deposed that it had been he who arranged for Mabel Gordon's visit to Aston. Surgeon Green of Leeds then gave evidence that Mabel Gordon had been five months pregnant at the time of the abortion. The sixth and last witness was Detective Inspector Ravenhall, who described Hindson's arrest.

The defence counsel, Hugo Young, tried to persuade the judge that there was no direct evidence against the prisoner and that the murder charge should be dropped. The judge ruled that the case was strong enough to go before a jury and after Mr Soden had summed up for the prosecution, Mr Young spoke for the defence. He said that the court was one of law rather than of morality and that there was no direct evidence that Hindson knew about the abortion.

The judge summed up saying that where a man procured an abortion for a woman who died as a result, the offence was murder. The all male jury took fifteen minutes to convict the prisoner of murder but recommended mercy, saying that they were 'very sorry for the prisoner'. The judge then condemned Hindson to death.

Although there was less open public sympathy for Hindson than there had been for Mrs Eden, it was realised that a hanging would be inappropriate. Hindson himself denied widespread reports that Mabel Gordon's aborted child was his and said that he had just been doing an unfortunate woman what he imagined was a favour. On 17 March 1896, he was reprieved and his sentence was commuted to hard labour for life.

This case leaves several mysteries. How many women had Mrs

Eden aborted and with what results? Had she just started on her career in October 1895 or was she a veteran abortionist? Did Thomas Simister know about his wife's abortion beforehand and would she have survived another childbirth anyway? John Hindson was certainly a rat but was Mabel Gordon his mistress or was he merely, for once in his, life acting out of sympathy for a woman in trouble?

Much of Aston and Handsworth remain as they were in 1895. For instance, the *Barton Arms*, where the inquest on Rebecca Simister was held, survives today as a pub-cum-Thai restaurant. There is still an *Albion Hotel* in Leeds.

CHAPTER 20

Who Killed Lucy Askham?

Nuneaton, 1913

In 1913, James Williams was a travelling artist who exhibited and sold his paintings on any convenient pavement. His age is mentioned nowhere in press accounts of the Lucy Askham case but the *Nuneaton Chronicle* of 9 May 1913 described him as 'a tall gaunt man with hair turning grey.'

For ten years, Williams had lived with Lucy Askham, a water-colour artist who sold her pictures door to door having a hawker's license. In 1913 she was thirty-eight. Her parents having died, her nearest living relative was her brother, a Cambridge master fruiterer with whom she was rarely in contact.

James and Lucy had never married. James was Roman Catholic and was to claim that they had never married because he could not persuade Lucy to convert to Catholicism. More probably it was because such relationships were far more common among artists than they were generally. Today' living together without getting married is so routine that few people raise an eyelid but in 1913 it was very different. The Williams-Askham relationship was childless.

On Saturday 15 March 1913' James and Lucy had been renting a first floor room, for the previous six weeks, for five shillings a week, from Mrs Ada Giles Duckett of 16 Vicarage Street Nuneaton. They found their own light and food and were a 'peaceable' couple who Mrs Duckett never heard swear. James would return at eleven at night and Lucy would often return at midnight, sometimes the worse for drink. The couple's living together and Lucy's late returns initially made Mrs Duckett suspicious but she realised her lodgers' basic good character and once Lucy explained that she had missed the last tram from Bedworth. In any case, few landladies would sniff at five shillings a week.

At about ten in the morning on Saturday 15 March 1913, James Williams left Mrs Duckett's. He walked to Cash's Lane off the Foleshill Road on the north side of Coventry, nine miles south of Nuneaton, where he exhibited his pictures on the pavement. He never saw Lucy alive again. At about half twelve in the afternoon, Lucy left Mrs Duckett's to sell her pictures door to door. At about eight in the evening, she sold a sketch of John Bunyan's Cottage, for one and sixpence, to Florence Cornell a Sketchley woman. Sketchley was then a hamlet about four miles north of Nuneaton and on the edge of Hinckley. John Bunyan was a seventeenth century Bedfordshire puritan preacher and author of *Pilgrim's Progress*.

Meanwhile, James Williams stayed at Cash's Lane from two in the afternoon to nine at night. Having made about ten shillings, he paid three-pence and rode on the tram back to Bedworth. He then walked back to his Nuneaton lodgings without stopping in any pubs on the way. He got back at twenty to eleven and went to his room. He got the fire going and put the kettle on. At twelve midnight he heard Mrs Duckett come up to bed. They spoke and he told her about his concern for Lucy.

James Williams stayed up waiting for Lucy until five in the morning feeling both angry thinking that she was stopping out late, and concerned. He then went to bed, getting up at half past ten in the morning on Sunday 16 March. At about eleven am two youths, William Joseph Wills, aged twenty-one, of Midland Road, and William Hardy, sixteen, of Gadsby Road, were walking their terrier on Nuneaton's Hinckley Road. The dog became excited about something in the two foot deep, rain-swollen, ditch and thinking it was after a rabbit the youths followed it. They found a middle-aged woman's corpse whose throat had been cut. Despite heavy rain the previous night the area round the body was blood-soaked.

A crowd soon arrived and local man, Walter Coles, went to Mr Yoxall's house where the nearest telephone was and rang the police. Inspector Saunders, Detective Sergeant Mason and PCs Mobley and Smith arrived. The body was taken to the Nuneaton Police Mortuary. In its pockets were found two shillings, four pence halfpenny, some potted meat, cakes and other food. Heavy rain that night and sightseers' trampling feet had obliterated all footmarks but the victim's body had clearly been moved.

At about twelve noon that Sunday, James Williams met Mrs Duckett and paid her two and six (his share of the rent). Distorted word had spread about the two youths' discovery and Mrs Duckett told Williams that a woman's body had been found, having apparently been killed in a motor accident, a growing problem in 1913. Williams contacted the police and recognised and identified Lucy's body in the mortuary.

Dr William Nason did a post-mortem on Lucy's corpse, on

Sunday afternoon. Her throat had been cut and the wound was seven inches long. It had cut the jugular vein and had pierced the bone to a depth of a quarter of an inch. Great force must have been used and the death could not possibly have been suicide or a motor accident. Dr Nason estimated that the victim had been killed at between nine in the evening and twelve midnight on the night of Saturday 15 March 1913.

On the afternoon of Tuesday 18 March 1913, an inquest into the victim's death was opened at the Nuneaton Law Courts. The only witness that day was James Williams, who described his movements on the day of the murder and identified the body. The inquest then adjourned to await further police inquiries. On Saturday 22 March 1913, Lucy Askham was buried at Nuneaton Cemetery, her funeral being paid for by the parish authorities.

Meanwhile, the police investigated. One strong suspect was, naturally, James Williams, but his alibi held up. A massive red herring was provided by Florence Rose Long, the wife of Frank Long, a blind Nuneaton street musician. She claimed to have seen a man and a woman quarrelling in the street at half ten at night on Saturday the 15th in Nuneaton. The man apparently blamed the woman for having only made three shillings, four-pence, half-penny that day and said that this was not enough.

At about midnight, Florence claimed that she saw the man, whom she had seen earlier, cut the woman's throat and say: 'There I've done you in now you b......' He then saw Florence and said: 'If you split I'll finish you.'

On Tuesday 18 March 1913, Florence Long met a Mrs Proctor of 3 Twitchell Yard Nuneaton in Mrs Proctor's washhouse. They were probably related because Florence's parents were Thomas and Sarah Proctor who also lived in Twitchell Yard. Florence told Mrs Proctor that she had seen the murder and Mrs Proctor replied: 'Keep your mouth shut Florrie!' Sarah Proctor also gave her daughter similar advice.

Florence Long had a long criminal record, having been seven times convicted for drunkenness and twice for attempted suicide. On Tuesday 23 April, she was arrested for drunkenness at Atherstone. She told Inspector Spencer of the Atherstone police about what she had allegedly seen saying that she had finally got back to her temporary lodgings at Mrs Blowers's in Hinckley at two in the morning on Sunday 16 March 1913. Despite providing this information, Florence was sentenced to two weeks in prison for drunkenness and repeated her story to the Warwick Gaol authorities.

The police were highly suspicious of this evidence. They

discovered that, according to Mrs Blower of Harrold Square, Hinckley, and her daughter Florence May Blower, Florence Long had left Nuneaton for Hinckley on the half past seven evening train on Saturday 15 March and stayed at their Harrold Square home all night, having supper at eleven at night.

Florence Long's own mother, Sarah Proctor, told the police that her daughter was a congenital liar and that 'she could not believe her in anything'. Further police research discovered that Florence Long had lived with another man whose surname was Williams. They had separated after Florence refused to become a prostitute for him and he had threatened to kill her. Also on Tuesday 18 March, Inspector Jackson of the Warwick police, who had been helping the Nuneaton police with their inquiries, had met Florence Long near Hinckley. She had denied all knowledge of the murder. Although this denial might have been made out of fear it greatly weakened her later evidence.

Having cleared James Williams, despite this red herring, the police decided that Lucy Askham had been killed by someone whose sexual advances she had resisted and who had then fled the scene. In particular, on the night of Saturday 15 March 1913, a man took lodgings at a Hinckley lodging house. He was 'excited and agitated' and his left hand was bandaged with a handkerchief. He barely touched his supper before retiring to bed. The next morning it was discovered that he had fled through an open bathroom window.

The police sent the following wanted person's description to police stations across Britain. It described a suspect:

> . . . *aged 44 or 45 years, height 5ft 7 or 8 inches , thin face, slight light moustache, wearing a dark cloth cap, turn down collar and has his left hand bandaged, who on the night of 15th of March took lodgings at a common lodging house at Hinckley and left sometime during the night by getting through the bathroom window. This man may have blood on some of his clothing.*

This man was presumably the killer. He may or may not have been the man who sold a razor in a case to Mr J Bailey at the *King William Inn* on the Coton Road, Nuneaton on Sunday 16 March 1913. The razor was spotless though it might have been cleaned and it was not until Thursday 20 March that Mr Bailey thought to contact the police.

The police, having exhausted all lines of inquiry, the adjourned inquest resumed on Tuesday 6 May 1913. James Williams was the first witness and was questioned thoroughly as to his movements

The King William where in March 1913 'a mysterious stranger' sold a newly cleaned razor. The author

on the weekend of the murder and as to his relations with the victim. He said that they had, for ten years, lived 'a most peaceful life and they had no serious quarrel between them at any time'. He had been worried about her habit of staying out late at night fearing that she might be attacked.

The next witness, Mrs Duckett, corroborated the previous witness's account of his return home on the night of the murder and was questioned as to relations between James and Lucy. She denied that James Williams had ever 'knocked the deceased about'.

Florence Cornell, the Sketchley woman to whom the victim had sold a picture, gave her evidence that she had seen the deceased at eight o'clock on the night of the murder. William Harding then described having found the body and Inspector Saunders, who had led the police who were called to the murder scene, gave his evidence.

The sixth witness was Florence Long. She was allowed to give her evidence in full but then Mrs Blower and her daughter testified that at the time she supposedly witnessed the murder Florence Long had been at the Blowers' house. Florence failed to recognise James Williams from among a group of other men who stood up at the inquest.

The inquest then adjourned again and reopened the next day, Wednesday 7 May 1913. Mrs Proctor testified that Florence Long had told her about having seen the murder and that in reply Mrs Proctor had told her to shut up. Florence Long's mother, Sarah Proctor, gave evidence that Florence had told her about the murder but had not been believed because her daughter was a congenital liar with a long criminal record.

Inspector Spencer of the Atherstone police testified as to what Florence Long had told him. Mrs Blower repeated her earlier evidence as to Florence Long's being at her house when she had supposedly been witnessing the murder.

Florence Long then repeated her earlier claims but the coroner explained about how Florence imagined that James Williams was in fact another Williams who was Florence's ex-boyfriend. The tenth witness was Inspector Jackson of the Warwick police who described how on Tuesday 18 March Florence Long had denied seeing the murder.

Nuneaton Cemetery where Lucy Askham was buried in a pauper's grave.
The author

The eleventh and last witness, Surgeon William Nason, described how the victim's throat had been cut at sometime between nine and twelve on the night of Saturday 15 March. The coroner then summed up explaining that James Williams had proved his alibi. The coroner's jury took ten minutes to return a verdict that the victim had been 'murdered by a person or persons unknown'.

Whoever killed Lucy Askham is almost certainly long dead. In theory the killer could be a sixteen-year-old who at the time of writing (2005) is 108 but this seems unlikely. Perhaps someone, somewhere, knows who killed the unfortunate Lucy Askham?

Nuneaton Borough Council is good at providing historic information for visitors but Nuneaton was and is a working industrial and commercial centre rather than a tourist town. Nevertheless, a great many buildings remain there that were present in 1913.

CHAPTER 21

The Belgian Asylum Seeker

Birmingham, 1918

In August 1914, the Kaiser's Germany started the First World War by invading Belgium in violation of its treaty obligations which the German Chancellor Von Bethmann Hollweg dismissed as a 'scrap of paper'. When the Belgians dared to fiercely defend their country the Germans committed many atrocities in both hot and cold blood. Also, there were the inevitable fake atrocity stories. More than a quarter of a million Belgians fled to Britain and about 4,500 came to Birmingham. Among the Belgian refugees or asylum seekers, as we would call them, who came to Birmingham were Pierre Axel Verelst and his thirty-two-year-old wife, Clemence who arrived in May 1915. They had fled from Belgium earlier but came to Birmingham so that Pierre could work in Birmingham's booming munitions industry. Having made enough money, they moved to London and opened a teashop.

Clemence fell in love with one of the teashop's customers, thirty-one-year old fellow Belgian refugee and skilled toolmaker Louis Van de Kerkhove, who came from an Antwerp suburb. Louis and Clemence moved to Birmingham, Louis getting a job at Austin's Longbridge factory. The relationship was stormy and they soon split. Clemence took lodgings with a fellow Belgian refugee, Mrs Catherine Johansson, of 248 Windsor Street in Nechells, Birmingham who had been in the city since September 1914. Clemence obtained work first as a munitions worker, and then as a waitress at Brun's Coffee House in Dale End, while Louis moved to Dudley.

On Sunday 13 January 1918, Louis visited his ex-lover at Brun's Coffee House. To avoid a scene Clemence left work early. Later that evening at about seven a fellow waitress, Hilda Tudor, saw Louis and Clemence talking in a foreign language, presumably one of Belgium's two languages, Walloon-French or Flemish, at the *White Horse Hotel* at 30 Congreve Street. Louis drank 'plenty of whisky'.

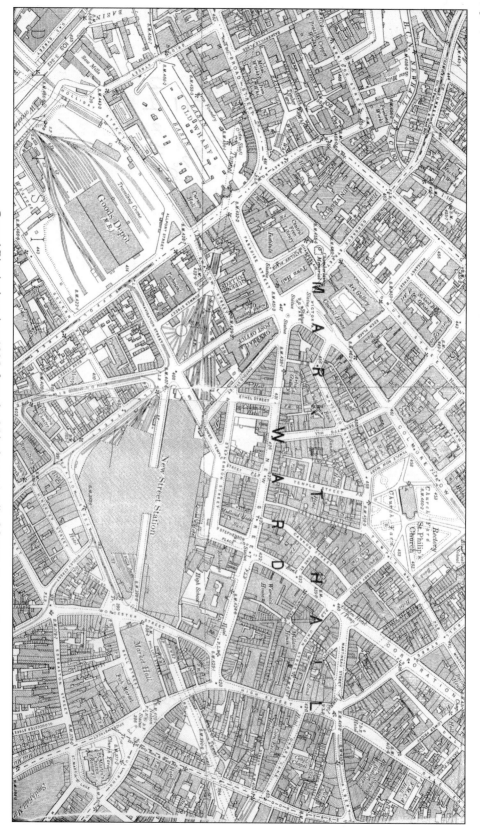

Central Birmingham in c.1905, from the 25 inches to 1 mile OS map. Ordnance Survey

At about nine the same evening, Louis and Clemence booked a room for the night at the *Shaftesbury Temperance Hotel* at 61 Station Street, Birmingham, which was kept by a husband and wife Samuel and Mary Carey. Louis told Mary Carey that Clemence was his wife and a chambermaid Florence Powers showed the couple to their room.

Some time after Louis and Clemence had gone to their room, two chambermaids, Pauline Hyman and Sarah Rosenthal, heard groans and sounds of violence coming from it. They summoned help and the hotel's assistant boots, James Kilkenny, and Lawrence Hughes, a naval signalman visiting a friend who was a guest at the Shaftesbury, came to see what was up and heard Clemence shout: 'He's murdering me!'

Kilkenny and Hughes knocked on the door of the couple's room's demanding entry. In response, a half-naked Louis came out, threw a clasp knife on the floor and said: 'I've done it.' The room was unlit but there was a landing light on and Kilkenny and Hughes saw Clememce crouching on the floor half naked. She crawled out of the room on her hands and knees and the two men saw that she had been repeatedly stabbed and her remaining clothes were blood-soaked. She exclaimed: 'God help me, I am dying.'

Clemence Verelst was taken to Birmingham General Hospital and Louis was arrested by PC Frederick Goodman who was called to the scene. At first it looked as if the victim might recover and among her visitors was Catherine Johansson. The victim told her friend that Louis had accused his ex-lover of sleeping with another man and had first tried to strangle her before repeatedly stabbing her. She also told Dr Edward Pearce, the General Hospital's resident pathologist, her account of events.

Louis was initially charged with grievous bodily harm. On being asked by PC Goodman as to his motive he said: 'That's right, she should not have fooled me about the same as she has done her husband.'

On 15 January 1918, Clemence Verelst died aged thirty-five. A post-mortem was performed by Dr William Clements of the General Hospital. The victim had been stabbed fourteen times. Twelve wounds were relatively slight but two were life threatening and the victim had finally died from a collapsed right lung and a partially collapsed left lung caused by her injuries.

Louis was charged with murder and an inquest into the victim's death was opened by the Birmingham coroner, Mr Isaac Bradley, on Thursday 17 January 1918. It heard evidence from Mrs Johansson, Dr Clements, Mary Carey, PC Goodman and Dr

Pearce before returning a verdict that the victim had been murdered by Louis Van de Kerkhove, who was committed for trial at the next Birmingham Assizes.

The accused was tried at Birmingham Assizes on Monday 18 March 1918. The judge was Mr Justice Alfred Tristram Lawrence who in 1921 was to be ennobled as the 1st Baron Trevethin. The prosecution was conducted by Mr Hollis-Walker KC. He was assisted by Sir William Ryland Dent Adkins KC MP who was Recorder of Nottingham from 1911 to 1920 when he became Recorder of Birmingham, and Liberal MP for Middleton, Lancashire from 1906 to 1923. The defence counsel was Mr Richard Willes.

Mr Hollis-Walker presented the prosecution case. Mrs Johansson, Florence Powers, Pauline Hyman, Sarah Rosenthal, James Kilkenny, Mary Casey and Drs Clements and Pearce gave their evidence.

There was little the defence could do. The continental defence of 'crime of passion' was not available in an English court though the defence did attempt to claim provocation. Despite speaking reasonable English, the prisoner testified through an interpreter. To quote the *Birmingham Post* of 19 March 1918: 'he said he remembered nothing of it. Afterwards the accused covered his face with his hands and sobbed bitterly.'

The jury convicted the defendant of murder and the judge sentenced him to death. The condemned man admitted the justice of the sentence but expressed hope that it might be commuted to life imprisonment as there was no death penalty in Belgium before the First World War. Two Roman Catholic priests, the Reverend Canon Robinson, who was the Catholic chaplain at Birmingham's Winson Green Prison, and a Belgian priest, Father Pierre Lipping, who came from the same Belgian community as the prisoner, gave him what comfort they could.

No reprieve came. Louis Van de Kerkhove was hanged inside Winson Green Prison on the morning of Tuesday 9 April 1918, aged thirty-two. The hanging was conducted by Mr Ellis who was assisted by Mr Brown. It was witnessed by the Under Sheriff, Mr Blenkinsop, the prison governor, by the prison surgeon, Dr Capels and by the Reverend Canon Robinson and Father Lipping. An inquest into the condemned's man death was opened the next day by Mr Isaac Bradley the Birmingham coroner. It returned the standard verdict that the prisoner's death was due to, 'hanging according to law'.

This case received far less publicity even in Birmingham than

Dale End in 2005. Not a single building remain there that Louis van de
Kerkhove or Clemence Verelst would have recognised. The author

did most murders especially those which ended in a hanging. The
reason is simple. Among the quarter of a million Belgian refugees
in Britain were inevitably some criminals, who took advantage of
the immense public sympathy for 'gallant little Belgium', and
wartime dislocation. This had produced a backlash which the
authorities had no desire to aggravate by over publicising such a
case. Incidentally the inquest received more publicity than the trial
and death sentence probably because the initial murder took the
authorities by surprise but by the time of the trial they would have
warned the press to play the case down.

Brun's Coffee House has long vanished and Dale End has
been completely redeveloped. The *Shaftesbury Temperance Hotel*
closed in the mid-1920s though the *White Horse* survived until the
mid-1960s when it was swept away to make way for the inner
ring road. The Victoria Law Courts, Winson Green Prison and
the General Hospital building survive though the General

Hospital's old building is the Children's Hospital today. Despite Second World War bombing and massive redevelopment, there are still many buildings, though far fewer businesses, in central Birmingham that were there in 1918. At the time of writing, (2006) a few very elderly people may have childhood memories of this case. Many more people must have known people involved in it.

CHAPTER 22

The Bad Copper

Birmingham, 1927

J ames Joseph Power was born in county Kilkenny, Ireland in 1894. After being a farm labourer he joined the Irish Guards and served in the First World War, being wounded three times. Afterwards, he came to Birmingham, working as a tram conductor before joining the Birmingham police in 1920. In 1923, he was sacked after he allegedly decoyed a servant girl onto allotments and assaulted her. He was not charged and the police got him a job at GKN. He eventually lost it and a period unemployed was followed by being a professional boxer. The police then helped him again and he became a warehouseman for Cannings, a Birmingham metal trade firm. He kept this job despite in May 1927 being fined £5, (c. £500 in modern money), for 'a common assault upon a young woman to whom his attentions were unwelcome'. By 1927 he was married with children.

On the evening of Saturday 2 July 1927, Charles Broomhead, twenty-two, a glassworker, of Devonshire Street, Winson Green, Birmingham, took his fiancee, Olive Gordon Turner, eighteen, of Ford Street, Hockley, Birmingham, who worked for Hussey and Dawson's a Ford Street aluminium firm, to the Winson Green Picture Palace, which had been opened in 1914. After seeing the films, the couple, who had been courting for nine months, left the cinema at about a quarter to ten at night, and walked back along the canal towpath near Winson Green Road.

At about a quarter to eleven, Broomhead and his fiancee were challenged by a man claiming to be a plainclothes policeman, who accused them of trespassing on canal property. He was big and well-built, and walked like a policeman, and the couple initially believed him and gave him their names and addresses. He asked for proof which they could not give so he said that he must arrest them. They agreed to go back to the police station with him. As they walked back along the canal the couple challenged him as to why he did not arrest other courting couples there. He said that one couple was enough. Eventually the 'policeman' offered to be 'squared'. Broomhead offered him four pence (about £3 by our standards), which was all he had and said: 'Well, have a drink.' Olive Turner also said that she had some money but at this point the 'policeman' showed the couple the three half crowns in his pockets and said: 'Four-pence is no good to me.'

The couple realised that the 'policeman' was an impostor. On her fiancé's advice Olive started to run home but the fake policeman ran after her. Broomhead pursued him but when he caught up with him the bogus policeman caught him by the collar with his left hand and punched him hard in the jaw with his right hand. Broomhead fell to the ground dazed. Recovering after a few minutes, he set out in pursuit of his fiancee and her assailant but was unable to find them.

Thinking that his girl might have reached home safely, he went to her Ford Street home where she lived with her grandmother, her mother being dead and her father living elsewhere. She was not there. Having contacted the police, Broomhead went to James Rooke's house. James was courting and was to marry Ivy Turner, Olive's sister. Broomhead and Rooke and other helpers, who joined them on the canal, searched for Olive.

Winson Green Prison and the nearby canal where the victim's body was found. The author

In the small hours of Sunday 3 July, the searchers found the missing girl's hat, handbag, and fur wrap lying by the canal. The police arrived and dragged the canal and at ten past six that morning they found her body. Her watch had stopped at eleven forty one. A post mortem was performed by Dr G W Cathles of Lodge Road, Birmingham, and Dr F W Lamb the assistant pathologist at the General Hospital, and lecturer in Pathology at Birmingham University. Olive had drowned and was unconscious when she hit the water because none was found in her stomach, so she had not screamed as she hit the water. There was a massive bruise on her forehead. The victim was still a virgin.

At first, the police were intensely suspicious of Broomhead, but corroborative evidence emerged to support his story. In particular, a courting couple, John Edgar Whillock and Doris Emeny reported having seen two men and a girl on the canal talking about money. Later the girl ran past them saying: 'There is a man after me and he will have you as well.' Willock, Emeny, and the girl ran together but the man chasing the girl caught up with the threesome. Claiming to be a policeman, he was again believed, Willock and Emeny standing by as he dragged the girl away.

On Monday 4 July 1927, the Birmingham police issued a description, based on Broomhead, Whillock, Emeny and other witnesses' evidence, of a man who they wanted to interview. He was: 'aged about forty; 5ft 10in or 5ft 11in in height; well built; clean shaven; having dark hair; wearing a dark suit and dirty light collar, believed to be soft; a dark cap; walks somewhat splay footed; and has rather a swinging gait.'

On Tuesday 5 July, the Birmingham coroner, Isaac Bradley, opened an inquest into the victim's death. The first witness was the victim's sister, Ivy. On the evening her sister died Ivy had been at the Reservoir Dance Hall, by Edgbaston Reservoir, and returned home to her grandmother at eleven. Ivy was woken at midnight to be told that Olive was missing. Ivy went to her fiancée James Rooke's house, but found that he had already left with Broomhead to search for the victim. The witness concluded by telling the inquest Broomhead's version of events as he had told her after the tragedy.

The second witness was Charles Broomhead. As he had a speech impediment his statement was read to the inquest by a court officer, and the witness nodded assent where appropriate. The third witness, Thomas Hill, a toolmaker, spoke of seeing two men and a woman talking about money by the canal on the evening of the murder.

John Edgar Whillock then testified. Drs Cathles and Lamb gave

Plan showing Lodge Road, Winson Green, produced for the inquest. Birmingham Library

the medical evidence and Doris Enemy corroborated her boyfriend, Whillock's, evidence.

The eighth witness was Mrs Caroline Leonard of 36 Brookfields Road, whose entry and the canal shared a common wall. She said that on the night of the tragedy she had seen a man come over her wall and onto her back path at about a quarter to twelve. She looked to see who he was but he quickened his pace fleeing down the street. He was tall and broad and walked heavily and wore a light coloured cap pulled over his face, and a dark grey coat.

Roland Bradley then testified. He had met Broomhead near the canal and had seen that he was badly bruised where the assailant had punched him. Arthur Leonard Bird gave evidence. He had met Broomhead by the canal at about half eleven on the night of the tragedy and was told: 'A bloke has just sploshed me.' Broomhead's mouth was bleeding.

The eleventh and last witness that day was James Rooke, who was courting Ivy Turner and who had been at the Reservoir Dance Hall with her on the night of the tragedy, before helping to search for the victim whose handbag, hat and fur wrap he had found. He explained that they had been dropped rather than placed where he had found them.

The coroner then adjourned the inquest informing the jury that James Power had just been arrested on suspicion of being the impostor. It was not clear yet what the charge against him would be but if it were murder or manslaughter the inquest would have to be adjourned until after the trial and any appeal.

After the adjournment, Mr E A Norton briefly spoke for the Birmingham Canal Navigation Ltd which owned the canal and feared a lawsuit. The towpath was private property as the company had been 'continuously endeavouring to make people realise' so it could not be held responsible for this crime.

On Tuesday 5 July, James Power appeared before the Birmingham Stipendiary Magistrate Lord Ilkeston. Lord Ilkeston was the Birmingham stipendiary from 1910 to 1950. As the Second Baron Ilkeston he was the only peer to be a stipendiary at that time. He was the son of the First Baron Ilkeston, Walter Foster, a doctor and Liberal MP, who represented Ilkeston, Derbyshire from 1887 to 1910, when he was ennobled.

At this stage, the prosecution was conducted by Mervyn Phippen Pugh who was Birmingham's prosecuting solicitor from 1924 to 1958 and who had previously worked for the Director of

Public Prosecutions, retaining his right to conduct crown prosecutions although working for the Birmingham authorities. In the First World War he had served with the Royal Berkshires and won the Military Cross and the DSO. The defence solicitor was Herbert Willison who, in his legal career, helped defend 110 alleged murderers of whom only seven were hanged.

Power was charged with causing Olive Turner's death and with impersonating a policeman. Mr Pugh asked for a week's remand for the police to complete their investigations. An identification parade was held. One witness had identified the prisoner as the man who had been seen with Broomhead and the victim, and another witness had seen the prisoner on the canal bank. Mr Willison challenged this saying that of six witnesses only two had identified the prisoner. Superintendent Penrice then said that of six witnesses, two had failed to identify the prisoner. Two had identified him and two more had said that it was either the accused or a look alike on the parade.

After some discussion, Lord Ilkeston agreed to a week's remand bail being refused. On Tuesday 12 July, the prisoner appeared again before Lord Ilkeston. The police requested more time to complete their investigations further evidence having turned up. A further remand was agreed and the prisoner was also charged with demanding money with menaces from Broomhead and Olive Turner. Mr Willison protested that the original charges were apparently not being proceeded with but he was informed that demanding money with menaces was simply an extra charge.

On Tuesday 19 July, the prisoner appeared before Lord Ilkeston again. Mr Pugh presented the prosecution case which included describing the prisoner's arrest. On 5 July, Broomhead and Detective Sergeant Edwards had waited outside the gates of Cannings Works at the corner of Birmingham's Kenyon and Great Hampton Streets. Broomhead had recognised the accused who briefly returned to the factory, on a pretext, before leaving it and being arrested.

The prisoner had claimed to be with a friend, John Davis, a Birmingham mill worker, at the *Beehive* pub on Cape Hill on the night of the tragedy. He had claimed to have separated from Davis at a quarter to eleven but had in fact left earlier.

Mr Pugh attempted to produce two witnesses, Edward Morris and Miss Frances Atkinson, who would testify that the prisoner had tried to pull the same 'arrest' trick on them on 3 February 1927. Mr Willison protested that this evidence was inadmissible but Mr Pugh refused to accept this.

John Davis then gave evidence. Power had left the *Beehive* on

Cape Hill at about ten on the evening of the tragedy. The two men had each had five half pints of beer. Power had been dressed in a grey cap, a darkish blue suit with a stripe on it, a soiled soft collar and a darkish tie. Both men had bought a rose from a waitress who came in the pub. They had stuck them in buttonholes. Power was wearing the same suit in court as he had when he had been in the pub with Davis.

Charles Broomhead then gave his evidence. In addition to his earlier account of events he remembered that the man who assaulted him by the canal had been wearing something in his button hole. Mr Willison then challenged as to how come Broomhead had described his assailant's suit as dark grey when the prisoner's suit was dark blue. Broomhead pointed out that he had seen it in very poor light and denied that Detective Sergeant Edwards had pointed out the prisoner to him at the factory gates.

John Davis's mother, Mrs Frances Eleanor Davis, corroborated her son's evidence saying that he had arrived home at about twenty-five past ten. A Birmingham boatman, John Godfrey, testified that he had seen a man, who resembled the prisoner, on the canal pestering courting couples, at about ten on the night of the tragedy.

Joseph Pym, the gatekeeper at Cannings, described how before his arrest, the prisoner had left the factory and then returned asking: 'What about the keys, Joe?' to be told that they were with the foreman who was still there. The suspect then walked away seeming somewhat 'upset or excited'.

The hearing was then adjourned for two days. On Thursday 21 July, it reopened Doris Emeny being the first witness that day, Edgar Whillock corroborating her evidence. PC Thompson described the finding of the body. Caroline Leonard gave evidence and next the prosecution attempted to call Edward Morris and Frances Atkinson. Lord Ilkeston ruled that their evidence was admissible but doubted its expediency and the couple were bound over in case it was needed at the assizes. They did not appear there but through the Birmingham press their story was generally known.

Detective Sergeant Edwards described the prisoner's arrest. In cross-examination by Mr Willison he admitted that another drunken suspect had been arrested but had been released when at an identity parade no witness picked him out.

Mr Pugh asked Lord Ilkeston to commit the prisoner for trial at the next assizes. Mr Willison denied that there was any case to answer and in a compromise decision the prisoner was remanded in custody until Tuesday 26 July.

On Tuesday 26, July Lord Ilkeston remanded the prisoner in custody again after a short hearing. That same day the adjourned inquest reopened. With the case against him moving forward the prisoner's interests at the inquest were represented by Birmingham barrister Percy Woodburn Williams. Drs Cathles and Lamb gave their medical evidence and Charles Broomhead testified as did John Godfrey, John Edgar Whillock, and Doris Emeny. On his counsel's advice the prisoner remained silent and in line with the 1926 Coroner's Act which had come into force on 1 May 1927, the inquest was adjourned until after the completion of the legal proceedings against the accused.

Meanwhile, the police had found more evidence. On Tuesday 26 July, a rape charge was brought against Power, and he was further remanded in custody until Wednesday 3 August when Lord Ilkeston heard evidence on it. On Monday 23 May 1927, the prisoner had allegedly met a young Birmingham widow and her boyfriend as they walked by the canal. Posing as a policeman, Power accused them of trespassing and demanded money. The man said that he was out of work and refused to give him any. The fake policeman knocked the man out and raped the woman under a canal bridge. She survived but failed to report the incident at the time perhaps out of fear or shame.

The woman's evidence was corroborated by John Calloway, a canal toll clerk, from whom the 'flustered and dazed' woman had asked directions home after the assault. Mr Williams strongly protested that such a charge and its attendant publicity would prejudice the defendant's trial but Lord Ilkeston agreed to let it go forward depending on whether the prisoner was charged with murder or not.

On Wednesday 10 August 1927, the prisoner appeared before Lord Ilkeston for the last time. Mr Pugh presented the evidence against the prisoner and the defence counsel was Percy Williams.

Mr Pugh explained that if an attacker caused someone to jump out of a window or into a river by actual or threatened violence and the victim died that was murder. However, if the attack caused a heart attack or stroke it was manslaughter.

Ivy Turner, Charles Broomhead, Doris Emeny and Edgar Whillock then gave evidence again. They all stated that the victim's face had not been bruised before the incident on the canal bank. Dr Cathles and Dr Lamb then said that exhaustion produced by frightened running might have caused the woman to fall unconscious into the canal, Dr Cathles saying that the woman was probably still alive when she entered the water. Thomas Hill testified again. Frank Pritchett and Mrs Florence Robinson who

The old Victoria Law Courts where the prisoner was tried. Birmingham Library

both lived near the canal gave evidence as to hearing terrifying female screams coming from the canal shortly before half eleven on the night of the tragedy.

At this point, the defence counsel finally realised the strength of the case against his client and tried to get the charge reduced to manslaughter. However, Lord Ilkeston ruled that it should be murder and the prisoner was committed for trial at the next Birmingham assizes.

James Joseph Power was brought to trial in Birmingham's Victoria Law Courts at the Birmingham Assizes on Wednesday 7 December 1927 before an all male jury. The judge was Sir Rigby Philip Watson Swift. The lead prosecution counsel was William Norman Birkett KC who was later to become a judge and Lord Birkett. He was assisted by William Eric Bousfield. The lead defence counsel was the Honourable Sir Reginald Coventry KC who had been the Recorder of Stoke on Trent since 1921 and who was the fourth son of the 9th Earl of Coventry. He was assisted by Percy Williams who had earlier represented the prisoner.

The trial lasted three days. On the first day, Mr Birkett presented the prosecution case in a speech lasting from shortly after the court opened at half-past ten in the morning until it adjourned for lunch. After lunch Charles Broomhead and Doris Emeny testified.

The second day, Thursday 8 December, John Edgar Whillock, Ivy Rooke (the former Ivy Turner), Thomas Hill, John Godfrey, Mrs Florence Robinson, Frank Pritchett, and Mrs Caroline Leonard gave evidence before lunch. After lunch PC Richard Thompson, Joseph Pym, John Davis, his mother Mrs Frances Eleanor Davis, Detective Sergeant Edwards, his colleague Detective Hewins, who corroborated the Sergeant's evidence, and Drs Cathles and Lamb gave their evidence. After having heard seventeen witnesses the court adjourned again.

On the third day the defence made its case. It presented one witness the accused James Power who spoke well. He said that on the murder day he had spent the afternoon at a cricket match before going to the *Beehive* on Cape Hill with John Davis, which they left at ten past ten. Later they walked past the *Yorkshire Grey* pub on the corner of Winson Street and saw its clock which said ten twenty. After chatting for five minutes they separated and at ten forty Powers returned home to his wife and children and their two lodgers. He went to bed at a quarter past eleven. He denied having told Detective Sergeant Edwards that he had been with John Davis until a quarter past eleven.

The prisoner said that he had seen John Godfrey, the canal boatman and alleged witness, before in the *Sir Charles Napier* pub or at least someone who looked like him. The defendant then said that the incident when he had gone back and asked about the keys at the factory had been a joke. Finally the accused said: 'He was a fairly powerful man until he was knocked about in the war.' i.e. the First World War. He currently weighed thirteen stones, having put on a stone in prison.

Mr Norman Birkett then made a concluding speech for the prosecution in which he said that it had been clearly proved that the prisoner was a murderer. This applied even if the victim had jumped into the canal in fear and in any case evidence showed that she was unconscious when she entered the water.

Sir Reginald Coventry spoke for the defence. He said that no credible motive had been presented since the victim had neither been robbed or raped suggesting that either the killer was a madman or the death was an accident. Sir Reginald said that Broomhead's evidence was questionable, saying that he had described the assailant wearing a dark grey suit, when the prisoner's suit was dark blue. He suggested that Broomhead was embellishing his story to help convict someone he imagined was involved in his fiancee's death. Sir Reginald said that the various witnesses' identifications were questionable since only some of them had identified the prisoner and the prosecution had not proved that the prisoner was on the canal that night. Finally, there was no actual proof that the victim had been murdered. She might have fallen into the canal accidentally while running away and her screams might have been in pain from being assaulted by her assailant.

The judge summed up in a one hour, fifty minute speech. He pointed out that the jury must decide if the crime was murder or manslaughter; and if the culprit was the prisoner or some other unknown man. The death could not possibly be suicide since the victim had been unconscious when she hit the water otherwise she would have screamed in the canal and swallowed canal water. There was no need to establish a motive before a conviction since killing a victim who had resisted rape was murder by definition. After going over the evidence in detail, the judge pointed out that the prisoner had not called his wife or their lodgers to corroborate his testimony as to his return home.

The all-male jury retired at twelve minutes to five and took an hour to convict the prisoner of murder. The condemned man said: 'You have found an innocent man guilty.' The judge then put on his black cap and sentenced Power to death. Power informed the court that he would appeal.

The prisoner's appeal was heard before the Lord Chief Justice Lord Hewart and Justices Avory and Branson, at the Court of Criminal Appeal on Thursday and Friday, 12/13 January 1928. Sir Reginald Coventry argued that the prisoner's trial was grossly unfair having been prejudiced by another unproven but widely publicised rape charge. There was laughter when Sir Reginald described Birmingham as a 'comparatively small place'. Lord Hewart retorted that 'the citizens of Birmingham would be a little startled to hear that'. Sir Reginald explained that Birmingham's local newspapers had widely publicised the inquest and magistrates' court proceedings making a fair trial impossible.

Concerning the death, Sir Reginald said that the prisoner had been elsewhere and that it might have been accidental. Lord Hewart challenged him as to if he was suggesting that the victim was a suicide and he denied this saying that the verdict 'Found Drowned' was a standard one. He pointed out alleged discrepancies in the evidence. For instance, Broomhead had said that his assailant wore a grey suit when the prisoner had been wearing a dark blue suit. The police had searched the prisoner's house and even dug up his garden in the hunt for a grey suit. John Godfrey's evidence was also questionable since he described the prisoner being on the canal at ten at night when reliable evidence said the prisoner was still in the *Beehive*.

Norman Birkett then countered. He said that the evidence against the prisoner was overwhelming. It was easy to mistake dark blue for grey in poor light and John Godfrey's time keeping discretion was minor since he was not wearing a watch. He pointed out that the prisoner had not called any of the available witnesses i.e. his wife and their lodgers, to corroborate his alibi despite having ample opportunity to do so.

The appeal was rejected. A petition was mounted for the prisoner's sentence to be commuted to life imprisonment but the Home Secretary rejected it. On Friday 20 January 1928, the adjourned inquest reopened and reached a formal verdict that the victim had been murdered by the condemned man.

At eight in the morning on Tuesday 31 January 1928, James Joseph Power, aged thirty-three, was hanged inside Birmingham's Winson Green Prison. The hangman was Thomas William Pierrepoint, the uncle of the more famous executioner Albert Pierrepoint. Two thousand people waited outside the prison gates to see the death notice posted. An inquest later that

Exterior of Winson Green Prison where the prisoner was hanged. The author

morning returned a verdict that the condemned man had been lawfully executed. A member of the jury asked if Power had confessed before he died but the coroner refused to answer this question.

With this case we have moved to the edge of history that is still (2006) in living memory. Lord Birkett was to go on to be the alternate British judge to Mr Justice Lawrence at the 1945–46 Nuremburg trials where Goering and other Nazi war criminals were tried.

Cannings, where the prisoner worked, has since been absorbed into the multinational but Birmingham-based MacDermid (UK) Ltd. Hussey and Dawson of Ford Street, where the victim worked, has a lineal successor, Hussey Gwenda Products Ltd of Birmingham.

The Winson Green Picture Palace closed in 1959 and the building has been demolished. The *Beehive* on Cape Hill has gone though several other Birmingham and Black Country pubs bear that name. The *Sir Charles Napier* on Rosebery Street, which was presumably where the prisoner allegedly saw John Godfrey,

REX v. JAMES JOSEPH POWER

(Appellant)

THIS is to give you notice that the Court of Criminal

Appeal has this day determined the appeal and application

for leave to appeal made by the above Appellant against his

conviction at the Warwick County Assizes Birmingham Division

held at Birmingham for the murder of one Olive Gordon *Turner*

AND THAT the said Court has dismissed the said appeal and

application.

Dated this 13th day of January 1928.

Leonard Kershaw .

Registrar of the Court of Criminal Appeal
Royal Courts of Justice,
London.

To
H.M. Coroner for the City
of Birmingham,
Coroner's Court,
Victoria Courts,
Corporation Street,
Birmingham.

The official notification that James Power's appeal was rejected. Birmingham
Library

closed in 1970 though another pub of that name survives in Gooch Street. The *Yorkshire Grey* still exists. The successor to the Reservoir Dance Hall was the Tower Ballroom.

Most but not all of the streets featured in this case still exist as does the canal. Second World War bombing and massive subsequent redevelopment have destroyed much of 1927 Birmingham but a great deal still remains.

James Power was almost certainly guilty. If by some fluke he was innocent his lifestyle had certainly been reckless. Apart from the evidence the police unearthed the Birmingham newspapers discovered other witnesses of his habit of posing as a policeman and pestering courting couples. Readers may sympathise with a man who had been three times wounded in the First World War. However, they should remember that millions served in that war. Probably because of his war service, Power had been given many chances and he had thrown them away. Lord Ilkeston and Mervyn Pugh were well known as firm but fair-minded men and the prisoner had a first-rate defence. Herbert Willison was one of Birmingham's toughest defence solicitors and Sir Reginald Coventry was a nationally known figure.

CHAPTER 23

The English Penal System

Τhis book covers cases stretching from 1800 to 1928. In 1800, George III was king, Napoleon's armies were rampaging across Europe, the Industrial Revolution was gathering steam, and the American War of Independence was recent history. By 1928, George V was king, Stanley Baldwin Prime Minister, Hitler was a rising German politician, air flight was routine, and Einstein had formulated the law of relativity.

This chapter looks at what the English penal system was like in the early nineteenth century, at how it changed over the period covered, and at some of the more recent changes which may affect how readers understand this book.

In the early nineteenth century, people suspected of murder or other crimes might be arrested on the spot by suspicious local people making a 'citizen's arrest' or they might be arrested by the local constable. If they were arrested by suspicious local people they would be handed over to the constable.

In villages and small towns law and order was maintained by unpaid local constables who combined policing with their regular jobs. Each parish had to have a constable. Some large towns had the first beginnings of professional police forces.

Once a murder had been discovered an inquest would be held as soon as possible. Until the inquest the murder suspect would be held locally. Some larger urban centres, such as Birmingham whose Public Office, housing the gaol and other facilities, was opened in 1806, had proper gaols. In other places people would be held in small 'lock ups' or even in rooms in houses or pubs specially hired for the purpose.

A coroner's inquest had to settle two questions. Firstly, it would have to decide if a murder was a murder. This was sometimes but not always easy. If the inquest decided that there had been a murder the coroner's jury would also have to decide if there was enough evidence to charge the suspect. Parallel to the inquest would be magistrates' proceedings which for all crimes other than murder, including then capital offences such as forgery, decided what prisoners should be charged with.

People charged with murder or other capital offences would be committed for trial at the assizes and taken to the assize town's gaol. In Warwickshire the assize towns were Warwick, Coventry (until 1884) and Birmingham (after 1884). Assizes were held twice a year, at Lent and in summer, and were presided over by two judges, sent out from London. Warwickshire was part of the Midland Circuit. Lesser crimes were tried at the county Quarter Sessions which, as their name indicates, were held four times a year and petty crimes were tried before the magistrates, then as now (see chapter seventeen).

Before the assizes began, a grand jury composed of well-off county inhabitants would meet to decide if there were 'true bills' against each prisoner, i.e. if they had been properly charged. The actual trial would be held before a 'petty jury' largely composed of people such as farmers, small businessmen and master craftsmen. There would be few rich people on ordinary juries and no very poor people.

The trial would be opened by a speech from the prosecuting counsel. Sometimes he declined to make one if he considered that his case was an 'open and shut' one. He would then call witnesses to prove his case. Once the prosecution had made its case the accused could make a speech in their own defence. Defence counsel were not allowed to speak on behalf of their clients in this period. The defence could call witnesses as in the Abraham Thornton case (Chapter 7) where eleven witnesses established his alibi.

The defence counsel – or the prisoner if he or she could not afford to pay for legal help (there was no legal aid in this period) – could cross-examine prosecution witnesses after they spoke, and the prosecution counsel could cross examine defence witnesses after they spoke. The judge could, if he wished, question both prosecution and defence witnesses after they spoke. A judge could use his right to question witnesses to discover the truth, or, of course, to help the prosecution or the defence.

Once the prosecution and the defence had made their cases, the judge would sum up the evidence for the benefit of the jury who might well be confused by having spent hours listening to evidence. Murder trials in particular usually lasted for many hours though not for many days as they usually do now. The jury would then be asked for its verdict. In this period juries usually took only a few minutes to reach a verdict, despite all verdicts having to be unanimous.

If alleged murderers or other alleged criminals were acquitted they would be freed, unless there were other charges against them. Convicted murderers were usually hanged on the second day after their conviction, or on a Monday if that day was a Sunday, but the judge had the power to delay an execution if he thought that there was some special reason for doing so.

There were a few cases where, due to special circumstances, convicted murderers had their sentences commuted to transportation to Australia. Also, sometimes murderers might escape by pleading insanity as did the 'Reverend' William Brooks at Warwick in 1812 (Chapter 6).

Many men and women were also condemned to death for offences other than murder such as attempted murder, forgery (see Chapter 4), armed robbery, violent burglaries, rape, arson, and other serious offences. Although most such people were, in fact, reprieved and their sentences commuted to transportation to Australia (Chapter 3), over half the executions in this period were for offences other than murder.

While convicts were awaiting execution they would be well attended and great attention was paid to their immortal souls. A Church of England, Roman Catholic or other clergyman would do his best to give them what consolation he could. Most prisoners awaiting execution freely admitted their guilt and even those who continued to protest their innocence generally announced that they had repented of their sins and hoped to go to heaven.

Executions were conducted on a gallows high enough for a large crowd to be able to see what was going on. The gallows were usually erected in front of the county gaol, though sometimes a nearby public open space, such as a common was used instead.

People who were hanged did not always die quickly, sometimes they were slowly strangled. The bodies of convicted murderers did not receive a Christian burial. Instead they were normally handed over to local surgeons or hospitals for dissection which would be watched by a mixture of medical students and ghouls. If people were hanged for alleged crimes other than murder their bodies would usually receive a Christian burial. Occasionally, the bodies of executed criminals would be 'gibbeted' i.e. hung in cages suspended from trees, or other convenient objects, in their local communities.

Murderers and sometimes other spectacular criminals would normally receive great local publicity but only sensational cases such as Abraham Thornton (Chapter 7) and Rebecca Hodges (Chapter 3) would receive much national publicity.

Perhaps the most important change in the legal system in the mid-nineteenth century was the creation of proper police forces. The Metropolitan (London) Police Force was first established in 1829. The 1839 County Police Act allowed for the creation of police forces outside London, and the 1856 County and Borough Police Act said that all areas of the country must have police forces, regardless of the attitude of local ratepayers.

The basic police ranks of constable, sergeant, inspector and superintendent were laid down in 1829 when the Metropolitan Police Force was established. Later experience led to the creation of the other police ranks. Provincial police forces came to be led by Chief Constables, a title which already existed in some areas before 1829, while the Metropolitan Police were controlled by a commissioner. Military style ranks, except for sergeant, were not used because of public fears that a police force might be a threat to civil liberties.

The existence of full-time trained policemen naturally made catching criminals easier, and the authorities were also helped by inventions such as the telegraph and later the telephone which made it easier to track down criminals.

There were major changes in the court system. One was the introduction of winter assizes, their creation helping to ensure that no one had to wait more than four or five months in prison for trial.

Between 1830 and 1862 the death sentence was gradually abolished in practice for all offences except murder and treason. Public opinion in general was strongly against abolishing the death sentence for murder but in practise an increasing number of convicted murderers had their sentences commuted to penal servitude for life, a sentence which replaced transportation for life, transportation being finally abolished in 1868. In particular, the execution of women became rarer (Chapter 19). When there was no question of a reprieve being issued, executions would be held within a few weeks of the trial rather than within two days as before.

In 1832, the practise of dissecting convicted murderer's bodies was abolished. The law providing for this practice dated back only to 1752 and had been unpopular with the ordinary people who, for all their faults, were more humane than their masters. Its abolition was generally welcomed except by ghouls. Instead medical schools were allowed to use the bodies of unclaimed pauper, whose dissection would attract less publicity. Gibbeting was abolished in 1834.

The 1836 Prisoner's Counsel Act, allowed defence counsel to

make a speech on behalf of their clients. Experienced lawyers could effectively put across their cases in such a way as to make their clients look innocent, despite the apparent strength of the prosecution case. Consequently, prosecution lawyers were forced to prepare their cases better, which meant that this reform reduced not only the number of wrongful convictions, but also the number of wrongful acquittals because of poorly prepared prosecution cases.

In 1868, public executions were abolished. This was welcomed by wide sections of the press, such as the *Birmingham Post*, but was doubtless opposed by the large numbers of people, from all walks of life, who had continued to flock to them, and by people such as baked potato salesmen and pickpockets who had benefited from the public interest in such events.

In 1879, the Directorate of Public Prosecutions was established and the first DPP was appointed (Chapter 18). Forty-seven years later, in 1926, the Coroner's Act laid down that when someone was charged with a murder the coroner's inquest should be adjourned until after the trial. This effectively ended the role of the coroner in most murder cases except for unsolved ones.

Five years after the last case to feature in this book, the Grand Jury system was abolished in 1933, though it still exists in the USA. The assize system was scrapped in 1972 and replaced by the present system whereby courts meet throughout the year to decide cases.

The death sentence was abolished in 1965 despite strong popular support for its retention. A friend of mine knew an old prison officer who said that he was a strong supporter of the death penalty – but not in any prison where he worked.

Finally, until just after the First World War, all juries consisted entirely of men and there were no women lawyers or judges. Nowadays, women sit on juries and there are many women lawyers and a substantial number of women judges.

Sources

Books

The Dictionary of National Biography
Kelly's and various other trade directories
Who Was Who
Murderous Birmingham, the executed of the twentieth century, John J
　　Eddleston, Breedon Books, 1987
Murder in the Midlands, J P Lethbridge, Robert Hale, 1989
Swing'em Fair, Coventry's Darker Side, David McGrory, Jones-Sands
　　Publishing, 1999
The Buildings of England, Warwickshire, Pevsner and Wedgwood,
　　Penguin, 1966
Warwickshire Tales of Mystery and Murder, Betty Smith, Countryside
　　Books, 2001
Dastardly Deeds in Victorian Warwickshire, Graham Sutherland,
　　Brewin Books, 1999

Newspapers

Birmingham Evening Mail
Aris's Birmingham Gazette
Birmingham Journal
Birmingham Post
Coventry Herald
Coventry Mercury
Coventry Evening Telegraph
Leamington Spa Courier
London Gazette
London Daily Mail
London Times
Nuneaton Chronicle
Nuneaton Observer
Rugby Advertiser
Stratford upon Avon Herald
Vanity Fair
Warwick Advertiser

Index

Places

Aberdeen 136
Alcester 69
Albion Hotel, Leeds 142, 144
Antwerp, Belgium 152
Aston (near Birmingham) 16, 18, 136–144
Aston in the Walls (Northamptonshire) 5
Atherstone 147, 150
Australia 12, 20

Barton Arms, Aston 138,139, 144
Beehive (pub), Cape Hill, Birmingham 163, 170
Binton Bridge 1
Birmingham 2, 13, 18, 19, 23–25, 44, 45, 47, 53–62, 63–68, 85, 88, 90, 93, 94, 103–113, 123, 123–127, 152–157, 158–172, 173
Birmingham General Hospital 154, 160
Black Dog, Chester 73
Bourton 95
Brailes 5–12, 26
Bringelly, NSW, Australia 20
Bristol 91
Bull's Head, Fordrough Street, Birmingham 103, 105, 106, 108
Burton Dasset 99

Cambridge, 145
Camperdown, Australia 20
Canal Tavern, Coventry 76–83

Castle and Falcon, Chester 73
Castle Bromwich 16, 41–52
Chester (Cheshire) 73
Coughton 69, 71, 74, 119
Coventry 2, 32, 76–83, 84, 88, 89, 174

Daventry 127
Deritend 17
Dublin 58
Dudley 49

Fenny Compton 98–101
Fillongley 27–36
Foleshill 81
Footherley 17, 18

George Inn, Lower Brailes 7, 9

Halesowen 17
Handsworth 139
Hatton 96, 120
Hinckley 147, 148
Hockley 62
Huddersfield, Yorkshire 123, 124

Ireland 53, 55

Kenilworth 76, 82
Kilkenny, Ireland 158
King William Inn, Coton Road, Nuneaton 148, 149

Leamington Hastings 95
Leamington Spa 95, 96, 128–135
Leeds 136, 139
Leicester 125
Liverpool 50, 54, 56, 58

London 15, 17, 52, 90, 91,127, 176
Long Compton 114–122
Lower Brailes 7, 8, 11

Macclesfield, Cheshire 86
Marlborough Head Inn Studley 72
Merrie Lion (Red Lion), Fenny Compton 101–102
Mulgoa, Australia 20

Napton 95
Navigation Street, Birmingham 103–113
New York, USA 123
Northend 99
Nottingham 141
Nuneaton 84–89, 145–151

Penn's Mills 45
Peterborough 91

Queen's Hospital, Birmingham 106

Red Lion, Long Compton 116, 122
Rollright Stones, Long Compton 115
Rugby 90–97
Rugby Tavern (formerly the *Windmill Inn*), Rugby 92, 96

Saint Chad's, Roman Catholic Cathedral, Birmingham 112
Saltley 14
Salutation, Snow Hill, Birmingham 64, 68

Shaftesbury Temperence Hotel, Birmingham 154
Shipston on Stour 5, 8, 10
Sketchley 146, 149
Snitterfield 1–4
Southam 95, 101
Southampton (Hampshire) 25
Spernall 69–75
Stockton 95
Stratford upon Avon 2, 73
Studley 72
Surrey 49, 63
Sutton Coldfield 18, 41–52

Tyburn House, public house, Castle Bromwich 41, 48

USA 72

Victoria Law Courts, Birmingham 167

Ward End 13–22
Warwick 1, 2, 6, 11, 15, 17, 23, 25, 27, 37–40, 48, 56, 58, 59, 63, 66, 73, 95, 98, 107, 111, 120, 121, 147, 150, 174
Washwood Heath 15, 16, 21
Welford on Avon 1
West Bromwich 123
Wheel Taven, Coventry 79
Whichford 6, 9
White Horse, Congreve Street, Birmingham 152
White Swan, Hospital Street, Birmingham 65
Winson Green, Birmingham 155, 158–172
Witton 43, 107, 113
Woolpack Inn Birmingham 55

Yorkshire Grey, Birmingham 172

People

Adams, Mr (1) 80
Adams, Mr (2) 108
Adams, Sergeant 63
Adamson, Dr GP 139,140
Adkins, Harold 55, 58
Adkins, Sir William 155
Alexander, Mary 8
Anderson, Mr JM 120
Ansell, Joseph 138
Arnold, Matthew 133
Arnold, Thomas 90, 133
Ashby, Detective Sergeant 125, 126
Ashford, Mary 41–52
Ashford, William 49, 50, 52
Askey, George 63
Askham, Lucy 145–151
Aspree, Thomas 43, 48
Atkins, George 83
Atkinson, Frances 163, 164
Avory, Mr Justice 169

Bacon, William 84, 86, 87, 88
Bailey, Mr 148
Baker, Dr John 91, 92, 95
Ball, Mrs Mary 84–89
Ball, Thomas 84–89
Barr, Ann 28, 29, 30, 35
Batkin, William 64, 65, 67
Bayley, Honourable Sir John 6, 9, 27, 33, 39
Beard, Detective Constable 107, 109
Bedford, William 47, 48
Bedworth, Joseph 17
Beere, Charles 99–101
Beere, Henry 99–101
Bellamy, Joseph 130, 133
Bennett, Mr 101
Benson, William 48
Bindley, Dr 65
Birch, Samuel 13–22
Bird, Arthur 162
Bird, Joseph 47, 48
Birkett, William Norman 167, 168, 169, 170
Bishop, Mrs Mary 86
Bishop, Samuel 86
Blenkinsop, Mr 155

Blenkinsop, Dr William 39
Blizzard, Joseph 15
Blizzard, William 15
Blower, Mrs 147, 148, 149
Blower, Florence 148, 149
Blower, Mary ('Betty Blue') 18
Boise, Reverend Ambrose 59
Booker, Reverend Luke 49
Bosanquet, Mr Justice 66
Boucher, John 16
Boughey, Thomas 55, 56, 58
Bousefield, William Eric 167
Bradbury, Sarah 14
Bradley, Isaac 154, 155, 160
Bradley, Roland 162
Bramwell, Baron George 116, 118
Branson, Mr Justice 169
Brinsley, Alderman 107
Briscoe, Phoebe 16, 48
Broadhurst, Thomas 44
Broomhead, Charles 158, 159, 160, 163, 164, 167
Brooks, Reverend William 37–40, 175
Brown, Mr 155
Buckinghamshire, Thomas 9, 1
Bullock, Joseph 25
Bulloes, William 16
Buszard, Mr 116, 121
Butler, Mrs 42, 43, 44

Calloway, John 165
Calloway, Sarah 8
Capels, Dr 155
Carey, Mary 154, 155
Carey, Samuel 154
Carey, Thomas 105, 108, 111
Carter, Mr 25
Carter, Benjamin 43, 48
Carter, William (1) 10
Carter, William (2) 82
Cathles, Dr GW 160, 165

Chamberlain, Inspector 95
Chamberlain, Joseph 107
Chamberlain, Neville 107
Chamberlyne, Mr 116
Chapman, Reverend Richard 88, 89
Chatwin, Mrs Elizabeth 109
Chesterton, John 44, 48
Chitty, Mr 50
Clarke, Mr 6, 25, 48, 66
Clarke, Daniel 48
Clifton, Thomas 8, 9
Clements, Dr William 154, 155
Clulee, Benjamin 64, 66
Coleman, William 49
Coleridge, Mr Justice 95
Coleridge, Sir John Taylor 84
Coles, Walter 146
Coltman, Mr Justice 80
Conway, Mary Ann 106
Cooke, Mrs Ann 37, 38, 39
Cooke, Joseph 43, 48
Copley, Mr 48
Corkery, Jeremiah 106–113
Cornell, Florence 146, 149
Coventry, Honourable Sir Reginald 167, 168, 169, 172
Cox, Hannah 42, 43, 48
Crampton, William 44, 48
Creswell, John 105, 109, 110
Crowley, Henry 72, 73
Crowley, James 69–75
Crowley, Joseph 73
Crowley, William 69–75
Cruise, John 109
Cunnington, George 103, 105, 108

Dale, Ellen 142
Dale, Thomas 48
Danks, Hannah 27–36
Danks, John 27–36
Danks, Sarah 28
Davenport, Joseph 63–67
Davies, Dr Birt 106

Davies, Mr Crowther 132, 133
Davis, Dr 109
Davis, Elizabeth 83
Davis, Emma 64, 65
Davis, Mrs Frances 164, 167
Davis, John 164, 167
Davrell, Mr 25
Dawson, Joseph 44, 48
Day, Mr Justice 140
Dennistoun, Mr 84
Devey, William (1) 63–68
Devey, William (2) 63
Dore, William 38, 39
Dorsett, Mr 140, 142
Dove, Dr John 10
Downes, William 105–108, 108, 111
Duckett, Mrs Ada Giles 145, 146, 149
Dugdale, Mr 108, 116
Dugdale, John Stratford 126, 127

Earl, Mr 26
Ebbage, Dr 100, 101
Edelmann, Alderman 132
Eden, Mrs Sarah Ann 136–144
Edwards, Detective Sergeant 163, 164, 167
Elkington, Elizabeth 35
Elkington, Dr Frances Russell 53, 56, 58
Elkington, Thomas 100, 101
Ellenborough, Lord 50
Ellis, Mr 155
Emeny, Doris 160, 162, 164, 165
Evans, John Henry 115, 118
Evans, Samuel 16, 19

Fairley, Dr 140
Farrington, Samuel 64, 65, 67
Field, Mr Justice 108
Field, Ann 5,9
Field, Mary 5–12, 26
Findon, John 72, 73
Fitzgerald, Mr 133
Fitzstephen, Mr 101

Flavel, Alderman 132
Fletcher, Sergeant Joseph 105, 106, 108, 109
Fletcher, PC Charles 105, 106, 198
Ford, Michael 53–62
Fowkes, Maria 76
Foxley, Bessie 125, 126
Freer, Dr George 47, 48

Gaillimore, Richard 14
Gale, Mr 73
Gamble, Dr 2
Gamgee, Dr Sampson 107, 113
Gardner, David 5–12
Garrow, Honourable Sir William 15
Garvey, Dr 138, 140
Gaskins, Inspector 101
George, Thomas 37, 39
Glenn, Thomas 82
Glossop, Chief Constable 107
Godfrey, John 164–169
Godwin, Mrs Ann 91–95
Godwin, George 91
Golsby, Ann 76–83
Golsby, Emma 76–83
Golsby, Mary 76, 77
Golsby, Robert 76–83
Golsby, Mrs Susan 76–83
Good, William 83
Goodman, PC, Frederick 154
Goodman, PC, John 105, 106, 108
Gordon, Mabel 136–144
Goulbourn, Sergeant 63, 66
Graham, Sir James 74
Grant, Elisabeth 125, 126
Grant, Susannah 23–26
Green, Dr Albert 142, 143
Green, Sarah 81
Greensall, Mr 44
Gregory, Richard 6
Grice–Hutchinson, Captain George William 141
Griffin, John 79, 80
Grooby, Edward 27–36
Groutage, Mary 58
Gurney, Mr 50

Hall, William 65
Hamilton, Dr Francis
    George 106, 109
Hamilton, John 110
Hamilton, Margaret 110
Hammond, Mrs Elizabeth
    37, 38, 39
Hammond, Thomas 14
Hardy, William 146
Hartwell, John 123–127
Harvey, Elizabeth 81, 82
Hawkins, Sir Henry 133
Haydon, John 44, 48
Haynes, Mother 18
Haywood, James 115–122
Heath, Mr 111
Heaton, Jane 44, 48
Helden Detective
    Inspector 123
Hemmings, George 15
Hewart, Lord 169
Hewins, Detective 167
Heyes, Mr 84
Higgins, Mary Ann 89
Hill, Mr 66, 73
Hill, Dr Alfred 133
Hill, Joseph 3
Hill, Thomas 160, 167
Hindson, John 136–144
Hitchen, William 25, 26
Hobbes, Robert 2
Hobbins, Frances 8
Hobdale, William 73
Hodges, Charles 20
Hodges George 20
Hodges, Rebecca 13–22,
    175
Hodges, William 15
Holden, John 44, 48
Holden, John junior 44,
    48
Hollis-Walker, Mr 155
Holt, Lord Chief Justice
    49
Hompidge, John 43, 48
Hopkins, Ann 87
Horner, John 25
Horniblow, Elizabeth
    129–134
Horniblow, Dr
    William`(1) 5, 10
Horniblow, Dr William
    (2) 129–134
Horniblow, William
    Henry 129

Hortin, Dr 47
Houghton, Mr 15
Hughes, Elizabeth 115,
    119
Hughes, Lawrence 154
Hughes, Thomas (1) 97
Hughes, Thomas (2) 115,
    116
Humfrey, Mr 66, 73, 81,
    82
Hutchinson, Dr George
    Wright 116, 119, 120
Hyde, John 8, 9
Hyde, Sarah Ann 105,
    108
Hyman, Pauline 154, 155

Ilife, Mr 87
Ilkeston, Lord 162, 164,
    165, 167, 172
Inge, Mr 25
Isaaacs, Superintendent
    James 92, 95

Jackson, Inspector 148
Jackson, George 44, 48
Jarvis, Susannah 76–83
Jenkins, John 108
Jennings, Martha 44, 48
Jennings William 44, 48
Joggett, William Peter 25
Johanson, Mrs Catherine
    152, 154, 155
Jones, Davis 81

Keep, Mr 140, 142
Kelly, Father 111
Kelly, Thomas 110
Kennett, Robert 25
Kenniwell, George 20
Kerkhove, Louis van de
    152–157
Kibbler, Sarah 129–134
Kilkenny, James 154, 155
King, Thomas 80, 83
Kynnersley, Mr 123, 125,
    126

Lacy, Ann 81
Lamb, Dr F W 160, 165,
Lane, Mr J 101
Laugharne, Reverend 60
Lavell, Frances 47, 48
Lavell, William 45, 47, 48
Lawley, Richard 65, 66

Lawrence, Mr Justice
    Alfred 155
Le Blanc, Mr 50
Le Blanc, Sir Simon 11,
    25, 26
Lee, Joseph 73
Leeson, George 64, 65
Leigh, Honourable EC
    101, 108–110
Leonard, Mrs Caroline
    162, 164, 167
Leonard, Thomas 110
Lines, Elizabeth 106
Lines, PC William
    105–113
Lipping, Father Pierre
    155
Littledale, Mr Justice 56
Long, Florence Rose 147,
    149, 150
Long, Frank 147
Lord, Mr 123
Lovat, Lord 127

Machell, Mr 42
Manning, Mr 119,120
Manning, Matilda
    136–143
Martin, Mr Baron 101
Mason, Catherine 15
Mason, Detective
    Sergeant 146
Mason, Ellen 139, 140
Mathew, Mr Justice 142
Maule, Mr Justice 73, 82
McNally, Samuel 110
Mee, Charles 110
Mellor, Mr 73, 80, 83, 84
Middleton, Dr Amos 10
Milner, Susannah 16, 19
Miller Mr 80, 82, 84, 88
Miller, Hannah 37–40
Mills, Mr 82
Millward, John 10
Mobley, PC 146

Moore, James 108
Morgan, Margaret 109,
    110
Morris, Dr 72,73
Morris, Mr 80
Morris, Edward 163, 164
Murrell, Mr 73

Nason, Dr William 146, 147, 151
Neale, Elizabeth 100
Neale, Thomas 100
Nevill, Joseph 80
Newman, Ann 5–12
Nicholls, John 72, 73
Norton, Mr E A 162
Nunn, Dr J R 121

O'Brien, Mr 95, 96
Odell Senior, Mr 79
Oughton, PC 99–101
Overton, Dr 79–82

Page, Deborah 29
Palmer Mrs 1,2
Palmer, Hannah 1–4
Palmer, John 1–4
Palmer, Mrs Mary 1–4
Palmer, Thomas 80
Park, Sir JA 63
Parker, Phyllis 6, 7, 9
Parry, Reverend 82, 83
Parsey, Dr William Henry 96, 120
Patteson, Mr Justice 82
Payn, William 13, 14, 16
Pearce, Dr Edward 154, 155
Penrice, Superintendent 163
Perkins, Mr 48
Perry, Mrs Hannah 53, 57, 60
Perry, Jane 16
Perry, Mary (1) 16
Perry, Mary (2) 53, 56, 60
Perry, Richard 53–62
Petty, Joseph 84, 85
Phillips, Mr 13, 14
Pierrepoint, Albert 169
Pierrepoint, Thomas 169
Pirie, Isabella 136, 142
Plummer, Charles 98–101
Poole, Mary 81
Poole, Mr E 101
Poole, WS 101
Potter, Miss Ellis 123, 124
Powell, Mrs Esther 125, 126
Power, James Joseph 158–172

Powers, Florence 154, 155
Pritchett, Frank 165, 167
Proctor, Mrs 147
Proctor, Sarah 147, 148, 150
Proctor, Thomas 147
Proctor, Hannah 29, 30, 32, 35
Prosser, Mr 79–82
Prouse, Dr 85, 88
Pugh, Mervyn 162, 164, 172
Pym, Joseph 164, 167

Queen of Scots, Mary 75

Rammell, Thomas 73
Ravenhall, Detective Inspector 138–142
Reader, Mr 15, 25, 48, 50
Redfern, George 17, 64
Reynolds, Miss 43
Reynolds, Mr (lawyer) 15, 26, 48, 50
Reynolds, Mr 43
Richardson, Mr 50
Richardson, Mrs Elizabeth 87
Richardson, Joseph 87
Richardson, Richard 10
Richardson, Thomas 8, 9
Ricketts, Thomas 98–101
Ricketts, William 100, 101
Ridley, Sir Matthew 141
Ridley, Nicholas 141
Robinson, Reverend Canon 155
Robinson, Mrs Florence 165, 167
Rogers, Aaran 105, 109, 110
Rooke, James 159–162
Rosenthal, Sarah 154, 155
Rowlands, Mr Horace 142
Rowley, Charles 63
Rowling, JK 122
Ryland, Edward 85
Ryland, Selina 85, 86

Salmon, PC 79–82
Sanderson, Mr 132, 133

Sandon, Thomas Charles Fitzhugh 25
Saunders, Inspector 146, 149
Seal, Detective Constable 109
Shakespeare, John 4
Shakespeare, William 4
Shaw, Professor George 85
Simister, Annie 138, 140
Simister, Rebecca 138, 139, 144
Simister, Thomas 138, 140
Simmonds, James 47, 48
Simpson, PC 116, 119
Simpson, Dr Patrick 30, 32
Slaughterford, Christopher 49
Smith-Soden, Dr John 32
Smith, Ann 57
Smith, Emma 109
Smith, Mary (1) 47, 48
Smith, Mary (2) 108
Soden, Mr 140, 143
Sowley, Sir George 48
Spencer, Inspector 147
Spooner, Mr 95
Squires, John 38, 39
Stanley, Mr 88
Stephenson, Sir Augustus 133
Stone, Sir Benjamin 141
Street, Joseph 72, 73
Swaine, Mrs 82, 83
Swift, Sir Philip 167

Taplin, John 9, 10
Tatnall, Henry 17, 58–60
Taylor, Alderman 107
Taylor, James 115, 116, 118
Taylor, Mary 14
Taylor, Thomas 73
Tennant, Ann 115–122
Tennant, John 115, 116, 118
Tew, William 37–39
Thatcher, Margaret 141
Thompson, PC Richard 164, 167

Thompson,
  Superintendent James
  116, 119
Thornton, Abraham
  43–52, 174, 175
Throckmorton, Francis
  75
Throckmorton, Sir Robert
  69, 74
Thursfield, Councillor Dr
  132
Tilsley, William 69–75
Tinklar, Captain 126
Tolkien, JRR 113
Townley, Lawrence 15
Townsend, John 81
Tudor, Hilda 152
Tupper, Mary 15
Turney, Ivy (later Rooke)
  159–162, 167
Turner, Olive 158–172
Turville, Reverend 59
Twamley, Zachariah 44

Underhill, William
  Maddocks 81, 82

Valentine, William 79
Vaughan, Sergeaant 26
Verelst, Clemence
  152–157

Verelst, Pierre 152–157
Vernon, Abel 87, 88
Vernon, Walter 106, 108
Vice, Inspector 79–82
Vickers, Dr 14
Voss, Ann 91
Voss, Elizabeth 91,93
Voss, Mary 91–94
Voss, Sarah Ann 91–97
Voss, William 91–97

Waddington, Mr 63
Walker, William (1) 15
Walker, William (2) 143
Wall, Mrs Mary Ann 123
Wallet, George 17
Walthew, John 58
Ward, Mr 87
Waring, Thomas 5, 6
Watson, Mrs Ann 80–82
Watson, Frederick 64
Watts, Thomas 84, 87, 88
Webb, James 65
Webb, William 58
Webley, Caroline 64, 65
Webster, Mrs Hannah 17
Webster, John 47, 48
Weeks, Edward 8
Whalen, Ann 106–111
Whalen, Thomas
  105–111

Whateley, Mr 25
Whateley, Mr J W 55, 67
Whillock, John Edgar 160,
  164, 165
White, James 44, 49
Wickham, Patrick 24, 25
Wilkins, Thomas 20
Willes, Mr Richard 155
Williams, Mr EL 63
Williams, James 145–151
William, Percy Woodburn
  165, 167
Williams, Thomas 15
Willis, Thomas 9
Willison, Herbert 163,
  164, 172
Wills, Mr Justice 133
Wills, William Joseph 146
Winter, Susannah 88, 89
Wood, John 13, 14
Woodcock, Charles 32
Woodcock, Francis 14
Woodcock, John 44, 48
Woodhouse, John 88
Wright, Mr 8

Young, Mr Hugo 133,
  134, 139, 143
Yoxall, James Henry 141